Public Law Perspectives
on a Private Law Problem

AUTO COMPENSATION PLANS

Public Law Perspectives on a Private Law Problem

AUTO COMPENSATION PLANS

BY

Walter J. Blum

AND

Harry Kalven, Jr.

LITTLE, BROWN AND COMPANY
Boston ● *Toronto*
1965

Preface

We would readily agree that the title we so carefully chose for this essay is somehow not quite adequate to suggest its nature and scope. Had we been writing many years ago—indeed well before the invention of the auto—we might have borrowed from a great tradition and called it simply "A Prolegomenon to Any Future Auto Compensation Plan." Had we been writing a generation ago, we might have followed a fashion and called it "How to Think About Auto Compensation Plans." And had someone not already used the idea, we might have entitled it "The Uneasy Case for the Auto Compensation Plan."

Any of these titles would have been closer to the mark. The point is that this is not an essay about any particular auto compensation plan. It is offered not to advance nor to impede any specific reform. It is an essay on basic liability theory and it uses the auto plan largely as a convenient strategy to limit the area to be covered. The essay thus is intended to provide an agenda for argument—to state the issues that must be confronted, discussed and resolved if one is to have a reasoned position on whether we should move away from the common law negligence system for dealing with auto accident losses to an arrangement which provides compensation promptly to all victims and does so without regard to whether anyone involved in the accident was at fault.

While the essay is written for all who are interested in auto compensation plans in particular or liability theory in general, it is aimed most pointedly at the law student. We have had in mind the possibility that it might provide a modest variant to the case method by affording an occasion, after the usual collection of cases had been read and mastered, for a comparably close analysis of the major policy issue in the tort field.

A brief comment about the overall organization of the essay may be useful.

In the first section we state the governing perspective and the rationale for this collaboration between a public law teacher and a private law teacher. We then turn, in the second section, to consider whether the question we are interested in is worth arguing about in view of the serious shortcomings so often charged today against the use of the fault principle in auto accidents. We try to show that, placed in proper context, these deficiencies are far from decisive. This leads, in the third section, to a consideration of whether argument about compensation plans is nevertheless academic because the existing system has already reached a point where only a very slight modification is needed to convert it into a compensation plan. In rejecting this thesis, we consider the weaknesses in trying to reach a plan through several short routes which tend to truncate discussion on the merits; these cut-offs include moving to a plan by way of the prevailing doctrine as to liability for ultrahazardous activity, the settlement practices of insurance companies, the acceptance of the compulsory auto liability insurance principle, and the analogy supplied by workmen's compensation acts. To complete the salvage of the issues we wish to discuss, we review, in the fourth section, the possibility of avoiding the whole subject by reaching a plan through the voluntary action of motorists in buying insurance which covers all victims. That happy solution seems not likely to be realized.

After underscoring that there are real costs involved in changing over from our existing system to a plan, in the fifth section we put what is for us the central question: what is the fair way of allocating the cost of the additional coverage called for by a plan? Four major alternatives are examined at length in the next four sections. The possibility of financing the expanded coverage by reallocating damages is dealt with in the sixth section. The alternative of accident insurance or an equivalent government welfare program is considered in the seventh section. In the eighth we investigate the possibility of financing the additional coverage out of the administrative economies expected from plans. The final alternative, that of putting the additional costs on motorists, is taken up in the ninth section, which focuses largely on what the law can learn from economics when accident injuries are viewed as costs.

In exploring these four routes to financing a plan, we intentionally underplay the impact which the insurance mechanism might have on the analysis. This aspect of the problem is given separate treatment in the tenth section.

In addition to broadening coverage for victims, a compensation plan has the objective of speeding up payments to an extent not possible under a system which predicates recovery on fault. The policy implications of this second target of plans are reviewed in the eleventh section.

Not until the twelfth section do we consider several factors which figure prominently in the ongoing political debate over plans—the likely impact of a plan on court congestion, the jury system, the trial bar and the insurance industry. On our scale these matters are entitled to weight, but only as by-products and side effects of adopting a plan.

Finally, in the last section, we attempt to summarize how on our view the case for a compensation plan stacks up. The assessment cannot be simple. The different approaches to financing a plan have underpinnings of unequal strength and they lead to significantly different types of plans. In the end, however, we return to an elementary observation: an auto compensation scheme, which basically is predicated on welfare notions, needs to be judged in comparison with an expanded social security system. And thus a plan, though it may initially seem to be a reform of private law, must be viewed from a public law perspective.

This essay was originally prepared as the 1964 Harry Shulman Lectures delivered at the Yale Law School in February, 1964. We are deeply grateful to the members of the Yale law faculty for their warm hospitality during our visit and for the stimulus of their invitation. We owe a special debt, too, to Professor Harold Demsetz of the University of Chicago who gave us generous counsel on certain points of economic analysis. Any errors are, of course, our own—or at least each other's.

WALTER J. BLUM
HARRY KALVEN, JR.

Chicago, 1964

P.S. We also acknowledge a great assist from our secretary, Florence Soble, who cheerfully endured the too many re-drafts of this manuscript.

Public Law Perspectives on a Private Law Problem

AUTO COMPENSATION PLANS

PUBLIC LAW PERSPECTIVES ON A PRIVATE LAW PROBLEM

AUTO COMPENSATION PLANS

1

A s WE prepared this essay we were acutely aware that our timing
was a little off. However we put our points, it would appear that
we were speaking almost a hundred years too late on behalf of our
views. We uneasily anticipate the compliment that in this piece we
will be showing ourselves to have two of the best minds of the 19th Century. But in any event our subject is utterly contemporary.[1]

In a general way we intend to discuss automobile accident compensation plans, but the center of our interest is somewhat different from that
of others who have written on the subject.[2] We are not responding di-

---

[1] The substance of this essay was presented as a series of lectures at the Yale Law
School in February, 1964, delivered jointly, although not quite simultaneously, by the
authors. In matters of style only slight effort has been made to correct for a certain
looseness which is characteristic of lectures. But in making these adjustments we are
anxious not to lose altogether an observation with which we began the lectures and
which may provide a clue to our stance: "Nor have we forgotten that the Yale Law
School is our host and that Yale students and friends are our audience: We are con-
fident that there is no group in America to whom the views we are about to express
will prove so little congenial."

After the manuscript was prepared and its title selected, our attention was called
to an article by Dean Leon Green entitled *Tort Law Public Law in Disguise*, 38 Texas
L. Rev. 1, 257 (1960). It appears, however, that he was using the term "public law"
in a somewhat different sense. And in any event see Kalven, Book Review, 26 U. Chi.
L. Rev. 679 (1959) (of Green, Traffic Victims: Tort Law and Insurance (1958)).

[2] Prior to publication we also had the benefit of reading a draft of Keeton and
O'Connell, *Basic Protection For the Traffic Victim* (Proposed Draft Dec. 1963). It is an
impressive and important contribution to the literature on the topic.

Although both essays are on the same subject, the center of interest is quite different.
Keeton and O'Connell have been chiefly interested in developing and defending a
specific legislative proposal; we have been interested in the analytic framework for
examining any type of auto compensation plan. There are certain points of tension
between the two presentations, but we have decided it would not be feasible to attempt

3

rectly to the practical problem of coping with carnage on the highways; nor are we concerned with the merits of any particular compensation plan. Instead our interest lies in exploring the underlying rationale of tort liability and compensation schemes, and we look upon auto accidents as providing both an active and a finite area for testing liability and compensation theories. Our concern therefore is with policy.

Speaking loosely, the main question is usually taken to involve a single choice between the common law system in which not all victims recover, and where inevitably there is delay in paying claims, and an auto compensation plan under which every victim would get something, including prompt payment of medical and emergency expenses.[3] This is too stark a contrast because of possible variations both on the common law side and among auto compensation plans. Thus if we add to the common law both compulsory liability insurance and comparative negligence—neither of which can now be considered a radical change—we end up with a negligence system under which the vast majority of victims recover something, albeit not promptly. And similarly if we postulate a compensation plan which embodies a low ceiling on damages, we would have a scheme under which victims as a class bear a large part of the losses. Moreover, most of the plans which have been offered resemble the common law to the extent that all losses are thought of as being borne only by motorists and victims of accidents. If we were to conceive of the special combination of tort law and social insurance of the English variety as constituting a plan, it differs both from the common law and from other plans in that the public at large, through tax funds, bears part of the losses. But enough has been said to indicate why our subject cannot quickly be reduced to a simple policy choice.

The idea of a plan for auto accidents has been conspicuous for almost

---

to deal with them at this time. Therefore we have allowed our manuscript to stand as it was.

There has been voluminous writing on the auto compensation plan theme generally. A reasonably complete bibliography is collected in GREGORY & KALVEN, CASES ON TORTS xliv-lii, 689-787 (1959).

Since 1959 there have been several articles that deserve special mention: Adams, *Law, Insurance and the Automobile Accident Victim*, 29 J. INS. 523 (1962); Calabresi, *Some Thoughts on Risk Distribution and the Law of Torts*, 70 YALE L.J. 499 (1961); James, *The Columbia Study of Compensation for Automobile Accidents: An Unanswered Challenge*, 59 COLUM. L. REV. 408 (1959); McCrae, *Legal Aspects of Automobile Compensation*, 29 J. INS. 185 (1962); C. Robert Morris, Jr., *Enterprise Liability and the Actuarial Process—the Insignificance of Foresight*, 70 YALE L.J. 554 (1961); Morris & Paul, *The Financial Impact of Automobile Accidents*, 110 U. PA. L. REV. 913 (1962).

[3] Even this generalization does not hold for all varieties of plans. Thus, for example, the "major medical" model, discussed in section 6, *infra* pages 32 *et seq.*, would not result in *all* auto victims receiving something.

half a century, with the obvious analogy to workmen's compensation having suggested itself early. The history of such proposals has been somewhat checkered, and may be quickly surveyed under three names—Ballantine, Columbia and Green.

The classic expression of the early enthusiasm is found in the 1916 Ballantine article,[4] albeit he was concerned with reforming the common law handling of railroad accidents, not auto accidents. His principal thesis was that "an altogether simpler method is available for the adjustment of . . . claims—a method based upon the ideas which have in recent years found beneficent expression in the workmen's compensation acts."[5]

The Columbia auto plan of 1932,[6] although still showing the impress of workmen's compensation, seems in retrospect to have been the offspring of two currents of thought—the emergence of realist jurisprudence and the reform enthusiasm which crystallized in the New Deal. The distinctive pitch of the Columbia plan was to launch large-scale empirical research into law in action and to sidestep the basic policy issues. The strategy was to overwhelm with a great array of hard facts which seemed to carry their own conclusions. But although the study immediately ranked as one of the great events in law, it soon disappeared from view, and this despite the fact that auto accidents continued to mount. Thereafter for almost two decades a period of curious inactivity set in, during which a whole generation of law school graduates probably never even heard about the Columbia report, and surely never read it.[7]

Today and for the past several years a revival of interest has been evident. The many distinguished workers in this field, including Fleming

---

[4] Ballentine, *A Compensation Plan for Railway Accident Claims*, 29 HARV. L. REV. 705 (1916). Other examples of early approaches are Carman, *Is a Motor Vehicle Accident Compensation Act Advisable?* 4 MINN. L. REV. 1 (1919); Rollins, *A Proposal to Extend the Compensation Principle to Accidents in the Streets*, MASS. L.Q. No. 5, p. 392 (1919).

[5] Ballantine, *supra* note 4, at 707.

[6] REPORT OF COMMITTEE TO STUDY COMPENSATION FOR AUTOMOBILE ACCIDENTS (COLUMBIA REPORTS) (1932). See also FRENCH, THE AUTOMOBILE COMPENSATION PLAN (1933); Smith, Lilly & Dowling, *Compensation for Automobile Accidents: A Symposium*, 32 COLUM. L. REV. 785 (1932).

[7] A notable exception is James & Law, *Compensation for Auto Accident Victims: A Story of Too Little and Too Late*, 26 CONN. B.J. 70 (1952) (a restudy of the experience in New Haven twenty years after the Columbia Plan); see the two careful studies by John F. Adams: *A Survey of the Economic-Financial Consequences of Personal Injuries Resulting from Automobile Accidents in the City of Philadelphia, 1953*, Temple University Economics and Business Bulletin, March 1955; and *A Comparative Analysis of Costs of Insuring Against Losses Due to Automobile Accidents: Various Hypotheses—New Jersey, 1955*, Temple University Economics and Business Bulletin, March 1960.

James,[8] Albert Ehrenzweig,[9] Robert Keeton and Jeffrey O'Connell,[10] Clarence Morris[11] and Alfred Conard,[12] will not take it amiss if we select the publication in 1958 of Leon Green's lectures on "Traffic Victims" as epitomizing the revival.[13] The striking thing about the lectures is not that Dean Green proposed an auto plan but that, after a long and brilliant career as a scholar in tort law, he argued strongly for jettisoning the whole traditional common law apparatus in favor of a simple compensation scheme.[14] Response to his proposal has made it clear that he was expressing the predominant attitude of the interested academic community.

The topic today is as lively as it ever has been.[15] Several factors may account for its re-emergence. The contemporary mood is again congenial to sociological research in law. It has seemed attractive to many to redo the Columbia study because the auto accident problem is a natural subject for large scale empirical research on which newly developed tools can be brought into play. In addition there is the enormous increase in insur-

---

[8] 2 HARPER & JAMES, TORTS, chs. XI-XIII (1956); James, *Accident Liability Reconsidered: The Impact of Liability Insurance*, 57 YALE L.J. 549 (1948); James, *supra* note 2; James & Law, *supra* note 7.

[9] EHRENZWEIG, "FULL AID" INSURANCE (1954); Ehrenzweig, *Towards an Automobile Compensation Plan*, FEDERATION OF INSURANCE COUNSEL QUARTERLY, No. 3, p. 5 (1961).

[10] *Op. cit. supra* note 2.

[11] Morris, *The Insurance Principle: Compulsory Insurance*, in CONFERENCE ON INSURANCE (University of Chicago Law School Conference Series No. 14, 1954); Morris, *Hazardous Enterprises and Risk Bearing Capacity*, 61 YALE L.J. 1172 (1952); Morris & Paul, *The Financial Impact of Automobile Accidents*, 110 U. PA. L. REV. 913 (1962).

[12] As this essay goes to press, Alfred Conard is completing a major study of auto accidents in Michigan, done jointly with the Michigan Survey Research Center. CONARD & MORGAN, THE ECONOMICS OF INJURY LITIGATION.

No list of commentators on auto plans would be complete without reference to Judge Robert Marx of Cincinnati who has been an indefatigable advocate of the reform for a quarter of a century. *E.g.*, Marx, *Compensation Insurance for Automobile Accident Victims: The Case for Compulsory Automobile Compensation Insurance*, 15 OHIO ST. L.J. 134 (1954). See GRAUBART, YESTERDAY'S LAWS AND TODAY'S ACCIDENTS (1963).

[13] GREEN, TRAFFIC VICTIMS: TORT LAW AND INSURANCE (1958); see Kalven, Book Review, 26 U. CHI. L. REV. 679 (1959).

[14] The first sentence of Dean Green's essay sets the tone: "This monograph seeks to demonstrate the obsolescence and futility of common law jury trial and liability insurance as a remedy for traffic casualties and advocates compulsory comprehensive loss insurance as a substitute." GREEN, *op. cit. supra* note 13, at 5. By way of conclusion, the author states: "The courts are powerless to reconstruct a rational process for general use. They have reached a dead end. As a means of giving adequate protection against the machines of the highway, negligence law has run its course. Something better must be found." *Id.* at 82.

[15] Within the past five years, the Governor of California has appointed a special commission to study auto plans. Dean Green and the team of Keeton and O'Connell have each formulated major legislative proposals; see notes 2 and 13 *supra*. Conard has made a major study of the existing processing of auto accident claims. See note 12 *supra*. And the Walter E. Meyer Research Institute has marked the area for major support. WALTER E. MEYER RESEARCH INSTITUTE OF LAW ANNUAL REP. 17-18 (1960-1962).

ance coverage for auto accidents. The ubiquity of insurance has sharpened the perception of the inefficiencies, costs and inequities of the present system for determining liability, measuring damages, and adjusting claims in or out of court. Another factor is the increased sensitivity to welfare. Concern has centered on the inability of the system to provide victims with prompt payment of their medical and emergency expenses. Finally, there has been the practical stimulus of urban court congestion which frequently has been blamed on auto accident cases crowding the dockets.[16] More than one seasoned trial judge has argued that an auto compensation plan under an administrative agency would be the best solution to court delay.[17]

Despite the renewed interest, current discussions of auto plans are largely unsatisfying. They lack any sustained confrontation of issues. The bar, although it might be expected to play the role of the experienced conservative and thus to supply a sharp challenge to the reform, has been bluntly hostile when not apathetic. At most an occasional spokesman has sallied forth in the journals to stigmatize the plans as socialistic departures from the American way of life.[18] And even if the response had been different, many would view with skepticism any defense of the current system by the lawyers because of the bar's great financial stake in its preservation. At the other extreme, proponents of auto plans, largely from academic life, have concentrated on social engineering to produce results they have already accepted as desirable. They appear so convinced that auto plans are the coming thing that they see no point in debating the merits of inevitable social change. Thus, although an appreciable amount has been written about plans, very little has centered on the kinds of policy issues which are to be our primary concern.

Indeed the special flavor of our policy concerns is the source of our collaboration in this essay. A bedrock question for us is the old-fashioned inquiry, who is to pay the bill? Payments to victims under compensation plans are compulsory payments under the coercion of the state, and obviously someone in the society must bear the cost. Allocating the cost of plans raises a fundamental issue of fairness. It strikes us as odd that this issue should figure so little in current discussions. The incidence of liability has been the classic question for the common law torts man; and yet the allocation of costs is simply another name for the allocation

---

16 ZEISEL, KALVEN & BUCHHOLZ, DELAY IN THE COURT (1959).

17 Compare Hofstadter, *Alternative Proposal to the Compensation Plan*, 1956 INS. L.J. 331; Hofstadter, *A Proposed Automobile Accident Compensation Plan*, 328 ANNALS 53 (March 1960).

18 Ryan & Greene, *Pedestrianism: A Strange Philosophy*, 42 A.B.A.J. 117 (1956); for a titular rejoinder, see Marx, *"Motorism", Not "Pedestrianism": Compensation for the Automobile's Victims*, 42 A.B.A.J. 421 (1956).

of liability. The oddity is that the common law torts man should lose all interest in the question when a shift is made from the common law to a compensation plan. We suspect we know the reason. Torts has been regarded as a private law topic concerned with resolving the disputes between particular individuals. But when one turns to insurance funds and compensation plans, the matter becomes alchemized into public law dealing with large groups in the society; and the result is that the private law expert has little interest in following through the questions which now seem to lie beyond the realm of his own special competence. Nor in their present stage of development have auto compensation plans engaged the attention of public law men, who have continued to center their interest on taxation and social security and other welfare systems. The topic has therefore fallen into a kind of no-man's land.

The design for our collaboration should now be clear. We hope to combine the perspectives of the teacher of private law and the teacher of public law on a topic that seems to need the attention and skills of both.

2

Anyone who wishes seriously to weigh the merits of an auto compensation plan is confronted with a peculiar difficulty: There is a tendency for the proponents to short-circuit the argument so that the question on the merits need never be reached. In brief, the difficulty is to get to a place where we can start an argument.

We begin therefore with trying to salvage the issues we wish to discuss. This requires that we meet two kinds of arguments which lead to the conclusion that no policy issue remains. One is that in the modern world fault has become so anachronistic and unworkable a criterion for liability that the common law system for handling auto accidents cannot be preferred to any half-way reasonable alternative. The other is that with the passage of time and for a variety of reasons our common law system has become so nearly equivalent to a compensation plan that there is nothing left to argue about.

We turn first to consider fault as a criterion of liability. We do so with only the most modest of expectations. The whole concept of fault, even in our torts system, is so closely tied to views on personal responsibility—and hence to values that have deep cultural and religious roots—that we must limit our discussion of it here to very narrow confines. We have no intention of developing an adequate brief on its behalf. Our purpose is merely to counteract the fashionable tendency to dismiss it out of hand as being an untenable principle.

There have been various objections to fault as a criterion for liability, but in oversimplified fashion they can be schematized as three general points:[19] (1) We can never get enough facts about a particular accident to know whether fault was present or not; (2) even if we had a full history of the event we would be unable to rationally apply the fault criterion because it is unintelligible; and (3) even if we knew the history of the event and understood what fault meant, we would be deciding cases on the basis of an unsound and arbitrary criterion.

The objection based on the difficulties of proof is a familiar one in all litigation, but it is urged as presenting special and decisive difficulties for the auto accident. There is the threat of evidence deteriorating because of the time it may take to get to trial. There is the sheer absence of competent witnesses at the crucial time of the event. And there is the emphasis under the fault criterion on split-second time sequences which place extra burdens on the capacity of witnesses to perceive, recall, and narrate.[20] These difficulties cumulate, we are told, so that the actual trial almost necessarily involves an imperfect and ambiguous historical reconstruction of the event, making a mockery of the effort to apply so subtle a normative criterion to the conduct involved. An impenetrable evidentiary screen thus makes fault unworkable as a criterion whatever its merits as a concept.

But does not this objection run the risk of proving too much? All adjudication is vulnerable to the inadequacies of evidence and the consequent exploitation of the situation by the skill of counsel. From prosecutions for murder to adjudications of the validity of family partnerships for income tax purposes, the law has had to wrestle with these difficulties. Auto accidents are at least more public than many other legal situations and they almost invariably do leave physical traces. The witness to an auto accident is asked for observations likely to be well within his daily experience. The law can tolerate a goodly margin of error, and the threshold of distortion which this line of attack on liability for fault must establish before it becomes a persuasive reason for throwing over the system is high. We remain skeptical that the evidentiary aspects of the auto

---

[19] EHRENZWEIG, "FULL AID" INSURANCE (1954); EHRENZWEIG, NEGLIGENCE WITHOUT FAULT (1951); GREEN, TRAFFIC VICTIMS: TORT LAW AND INSURANCE (1958); 2 HARPER & JAMES, TORTS, ch. XII (1956); Ehrenzweig, *A Psychoanalysis of Negligence*, 47 Nw. U.L. REV. 855 (1953); Leflar, *Negligence in Name Only*, 27 N.Y.U.L. REV. 564 (1952); McNiece & Thornton, *Is the Law of Negligence Obsolete?* 26 ST. JOHN'S L. REV. 255 (1952). As a counter tendency, see DeParcq, *In Defense of the Fault Principle*, 43 MINN. L. REV. 499 (1959).

[20] To take just one example, see Peterson v. Burkhalter, 38 Cal. 2d 107, 237 P.2d 977 (1951) (a last clear chance case in which the critical time interval is a few seconds).

accident are so peculiar as to be set apart from the evidentiary aspects of all other controversies that are brought to law.

The objections to fault as being an unintelligible concept also run the risk of proving too much. One needs a generous view of the meaning of a legal principle. We should be at least as charitable toward negligence as we are toward procedural due process, fraud, or gross income. All the big ideas of law are imprecise and have a core meaning which moves toward ambiguity at the margin. Except intuitively, there seems no way of measuring the relative clarity of such ideas. When we place negligence in the context of law's other big ideas, it looks at home. A simple test of its intelligibility is whether we can put easy cases so as to compel virtually complete agreement on the presence or absence of fault. We would all readily recognize that the negligence concept could pass this test were it not for the fact that our impressions of it are derived so much from the reading of appellate decisions with their marginal fact situations. The negligence concept, after all, has been employed by generations of lawyers and judges as though it made sense. They were able to argue in terms of it and to array cases inside and outside the line. The decades of apparently rational discussion at the bar are paralleled by the decades of law school teaching. Every law student has been exposed to the experience of locating the relevant variables involved and of ranking the cases through varying a fact in one direction or the other.[21]

But the critic can rightly say that law students do not decide cases, while juries do. The negligence concept is too vague, asserts the critic, to guide the judgment of juries. The result is that juries allocate liability on the basis of all kinds of legally irrelevant but humanly sympathetic grounds, and that the legal criterion in fact evaporates at the level of actual jury behavior.[22]

[21] Let us, as an illustration, take the well-known opinion of Learned Hand in Conway v. O'Brien, 111 F.2d 611 (2d Cir. 1940), an auto accident case. The defendant, approaching a covered bridge in Vermont, for convenience took a improper turn into the bridge so that he entered in the wrong lane and collided with an oncoming car. The plaintiff was a guest passenger injured in the collision. The defendant was familiar with the region and the prevailing low frequency of traffic; it was a local practice to make a wide turn into the bridge. Judge Hand decided that although defendant's conduct was negligent, it was not grossly negligent, as would have been required for recovery under the appropriate rule of liability to an auto guest.

On these facts; the urbane and ironic Hand was able to write an intelligible opinion. He was able to say, and we are able to follow him, that the defendant's conduct was neither without fault nor grossly negligent. Further, we can easily vary the facts and thereby alter our judgment. Had the defendant blown his horn and reduced his speed, we might well find no flaw in his conduct; while if he had made precisely the same turn on a high mountain road we probably would all agree he was grossly negligent.

[22] The recently compiled standard jury instructions for Illinois make explicit the full delegation of the negligence issue to the jury. "The law does not say how a

Normally on a point such as this there is little evidence other than lawyer anecdotes. However, in this instance the University of Chicago Law School Jury Project does have some directly relevant data.[23] In an extensive survey of the way judge and jury would decide the same personal injury case, the project found that in 80% of all cases the judge and jury agreed on liability or no liability. In 10% of the cases the jury found for the plaintiff where the judge would have found for the defendant. And, surprisingly, in the remaining 10% of the cases the judge would have found for the plaintiff where the jury found for the defendant. In brief, the jury would have found for the plaintiff in precisely the same number of cases as the judge.[24] The upshot seems to be that whatever hidden rules the jury is in fact following when it operates under the negligence formula, its rules must be very similar to those governing the judge. It is thus difficult to make any special argument about the failure of the negligence criterion to control the jury.

This, however, does not dispose of the issue completely since the critic may now press his final objection to the intelligibility of the fault principle—the difficulty of controlling even the behavior of judges by so expansible a standard as negligence. In fact he may well say that our Jury Project evidence confirms his worst fears that fault is inherently a quixotic criterion, that is infinitely expansible and is constantly changing its meaning. He will tell us that what is now regarded as negligence would have astonished judges and juries of a century ago. The challenge is that within established and apparently unchanging doctrine, the concept of negligence has greatly expanded its boundaries and will continue to do so.

The difficulty with this line of objection is that it presupposes that where a jury instructed under negligence has found negligence and the judge concurs, there is available the judgment of some third party bystander who fails to find negligence and who over time would increasingly be in disagreement with the official results. Without this ideal by-

reasonably careful person would act under the circumstances. That is for you to decide." ILLINOIS PATTERN JURY INSTRUCTIONS—CIVIL. No. 10.01 (1961).

[23] The results of this study are in the process of being written up for publication in book form under the title THE JURY, THE JUDGE AND THE TORT CASE.

A companion study of criminal cases is now at the publishers, ZEISEL & KALVEN, THE JURY, THE JUDGE AND THE CRIMINAL CASE.

For indications of other aspects of the jury project, see ZEISEL, KALVEN & BUCHHOLZ, DELAY IN THE COURT (1959); Strodbeck, *Social Process, the Law and Jury Functioning,* in LAW AND SOCIOLOGY (Evan ed. 1962); Zeisel, *Social Research on the Law: The Ideal and the Practical,* in LAW AND SOCIOLOGY 124 (Evan ed. 1962); James, *Evaluation of Expert Psychiatric Testimony,* 21 OHIO ST. L.J. 75 (1960); Kalven, *The Jury, the Law and the Personal Injury Damage Award,* 19 OHIO ST. L.J. 158 (1958).

[24] On the damage issue, however, it should be noted that the jury's awards average roughly 20% higher than the judge's.

stander how can one say that negligence was found by the law and the community when negligence does not exist? At a deeper level all that the negligence formula ever required was that the actor be held liable only when the community judged that the risk he took was not a reasonable one.[25] It is possible, although there is no evidence here, that the community is gradually becoming more stringent in its judgments about the reasonableness of risks in the operation of autos. In a formal sense no matter how harsh these judgments become the system would remain essentially a negligence system. In a realistic sense, however, it is conceivable that a point could be reached where negligence in auto accidents became only a fiction. Whatever might lie in the future, it seems clear to us that we are not approaching such a point today.

The third objection, that even in theory fault is an unsound criterion, has several facets. The first is that the law exaggerates the contribution of the actor's fault to an accident. On a larger view the actor's role is frequently dwarfed by other causally contributing factors, such as road engineering, traffic density, car design, traffic regulations, and the performance of other cars just before the accident. The precise challenge is whether an admitted flaw in the actor's conduct, looked at in the context of the other causes, is a sufficient basis for determining whether the accident victim is to get compensation.

This challenge appears to mirror the proposition sometimes advanced in criminal law that the individual actor's contribution to the crime is overshadowed by such other contributing factors as poor education, poverty, broken home, and so forth. The difficulty with this approach either in tort or in crime is that it is hard to see what else the law could do but single out the conduct of the individual actor. Speaking statistically, we can of course say that road engineering or broken homes are significant causes of accidents or crimes. But this does not help dispose of the individual case, and the law is charging the actor for a flaw in conduct that the mass of mankind—including those who come from broken homes or drive on poorly engineered highways—could have avoided. Although never philosophical about causation, the law has clearly recognized that any actor is but one of an infinity of causes of a particular event. It has dealt with the actor because he was a reachable cause and because his contribution to the event was relevant and decisive. Even if we concede

25 Compare the observation of Judge Clark in Pease v. Sinclair Ref. Co., 104 F.2d 183, 187 (2d Cir. 1939): "Hence we conclude that the conduct of both parties should go before the jury. The defendant asserts that such a course, with the corporate defendant here, means that a verdict for the plaintiff is certain to follow. Even if that is justifiable prophecy, it still does not mean that the jury is wrong or that a general community standard as to what should be the risks of the business undertaken by the defendant must be disregarded."

that the law always overrates the contribution of the actor, there is nothing in the auto accident field that gives this perception any special force.

The critic of the fault criterion might shift his emphasis and follow another line in pressing the point about the incommensurability of the actor's flaw and the consequences the law attaches to it. Negligence covers a multitude of sins, ranging from the grave to the trivial; and the critic can stress that there is no correlation whatsoever between the gravity of the sin and the magnitude of the damage caused. If tort damages were viewed as a system of fines, everyone would agree that the incidence of sanctions would be absurd, and it would be the rare case in which the punishment fit the crime. The difference in conduct between the negligent and the non-negligent drivers is too slight to support the huge difference in consequences that the fault principle attaches.

Does it matter for tort law that the punishment does not fit the crime? A sufficient answer is that the purpose of tort law is to compensate and not to punish; and this is well understood throughout the community and by the typical defendant. But the critic's point probably over-estimates the lack of correlation between risk and damage. On the average we are likely to find that the magnitude of harm caused correlates fairly well with the magnitude of the risk taken—in fact, the magnitude of the potential harm bears a direct relationship to the magnitude of the risk taken.[26] The critic's point in any event is especially weak in the case of auto accidents inasmuch as virtually everyone is well aware that an auto in motion can maim or kill. It is true that on occasion the law has recognized the point as when it limited liability for a slip of the pen in the *Ultramares* case.[27] The fact that no such limitation has been imposed in auto accident situations suggests that the law deliberately declines to follow the policy in the case of the auto. Be that as it may, it is improper to invert the process of judgment and argue that a small amount of harm somehow indicates a small degree of negligence. The key concept for the law here is risk; and what is constant in these situations is the amount of negligent risk taken—and this is a factor which, as Holmes noted almost a century ago, is independent of the harm that actually occurs.[28]

Another facet of the objection to fault as a principle builds on the not implausible assumption that all drivers are at some time or other clearly negligent. Most negligent conduct, however, is not actionable inasmuch

---

[26] As, for example, in the well-known "calculus of risk" formula of Judge Hand; see United States v. Carroll Towing Co., 159 F.2d 169 (2d Cir. 1947).

[27] Ultramares Corp. v. Touche, Nevin & Co., 255 N.Y. 170, 174 N.E. 441 (1931).

[28] HOLMES, THE COMMON LAW 79 (1881).

as it does not cause harm. Whether a given negligent act causes harm seems to be largely a matter of chance. Since all drivers are in the same boat morally and only chance distinguishes them, it has been urged that all drivers ought to pay for the damages inflicted by drivers as a class, and that it is unjustifiable to place the burden solely on those whom chance did not favor.

The popular impression that all drivers are alike in being occasionally negligent is very likely an overestimation, for it fails to take account of the many minor adjustments in conduct which are made when men engage in what seems to be essentially the same risky behavior. Driving eighty miles an hour is not a constant risk, and presumably all recognize that such a speed in the city entails a markedly higher risk than in the open country. But driving eighty miles an hour in the city does not represent a constant risk either, and those who drive at this speed under similar conditions might well do so with differing degrees of reserve or caution. It is not unlikely that there are grades of prudence even among the negligent risk takers. These minor differentiations in all probability partially account for which of the negligent drivers in fact get into accidents. And even if we grant that there is a large factor of chance as to which of the negligent drivers do cause accidents, it does not follow that the recruitment of drivers to accidents is a random process. Under the laws of chance, the drivers who take relatively more risks of a given magnitude are more likely to become involved in accidents than their fellow drivers who take relatively fewer risks of the same magnitude.[29]

The last challenge to fault as a principle echoes the recurring suggestion in much contemporary writing about tort law that a proper criterion for choice between competing rules is the sheer number of losses that would be shifted. We should always prefer, we are told, the rule that results in shifting the largest number of losses off victims. Using this criterion at the most general level, it could be said that the basic difficulty with the common law fault rule in the world of the auto is that it leaves too many victims of auto accidents uncompensated. And we are offered empirical studies to prove that this is indeed the case.

If the earlier objections to fault run the risk of proving too much, this one runs the risk of begging the question. It should be abundantly clear that the common law never has had information about the incidence of recovery which would follow from the application of its liability rules. What is more important, it has had no expectations about incidence of recovery, and could not have cared less. Its commitment to fault as a basis for shifting losses is independent of any estimates of how many

---

[29] Compare the accident proneness hypothesis; see James & Dickinson, *Accident Proneness and Accident Law*, 63 HARV. L. REV. 769 (1950).

losses will thus be shifted. No empirical study of gaps in loss shifting, insofar as they rest on the absence of liability, can be relevant. The striking point is that under the common law system it is intended that some victims will have to bear their own losses.[30]

As familiar as all this is, it marks a critical point of departure. The question frequently now heard is: "By what arrangement can we most expeditiously maximize the shifting of losses?" There is a profound difference between this and the old-fashioned question: "What losses should be shifted and what losses should the victim bear?" Under the logic of the common law, there is no meaningful way of answering the first question unless the second question has already been answered. We agree with that logic.

3

It will be recalled that we are engaged in salvaging the issues we wish to discuss. We have dealt with the first barrier to reaching the core policy issues raised by auto compensation plans—the position that the common law fault system is so completely unsatisfactory that any change would be for the better. We now turn to the second barrier—the propensity to argue that our present system is in operation so close to a compensation plan that only the smallest of steps is required to bring the law to a full plan. On this line of argument, any issue of principle becomes de minimis.

There are basically four points of departure from which it is urged that the present system can quickly be converted into a compensation plan: (1) use of our common law tort doctrine of absolute liability for harm resulting from ultrahazardous activities; (2) recognition of the degree to which settlement practices of insurance companies are realistically keyed to a rule of absolute liability in the auto accident field; (3) extension of the increasingly accepted principle of compulsory auto liability insurance; (4) adaptation to auto accidents of the long standing scheme of handling industrial accidents through workmen's compensation plans. We now explore in detail these four short routes to a plan.

The common law has never adhered to fault as the exclusive criterion of tort liability for accidents; the principle of strict liability, which has a familiar genealogy running from wild animals to *Rylands v. Fletcher*[31] to what section 519 of the *Restatement of Torts* currently labels as ultrahazardous activity, has always had a role.[32] In areas in which the

---

30 They may, of course, elect to shift the loss to an insurance fund by buying accident insurance; see section 7, *infra*, pages 40 *et seq.*

31 L.R. 3 H.L. 330 (1868).

32 For an engaging effort to state a rationale for this wing of tort liability, see Keeton, *Conditional Fault in the Law of Torts*, 72 HARV. L. REV. 401 (1959).

ultrahazardous principle is conventionally held to apply, if the law were to compel carrying liability insurance, the result would be a form of compensation plan. It would appear then that through the small change of bringing autos under section 519 and the additional small change of enacting a compulsory liability insurance law we would find ourselves with a fullblown compensation plan.

As a matter of technical *Restatement* doctrine, an activity is ultrahazardous if it "(a) necessarily involves the risk of serious harm . . . which cannot be eliminated by the exercise of the utmost care, and (b) is not a matter of common usage."[33] In the comment to the section, it is said that "automobiles have come into such general use that their operation is a matter of common usage. This, together with the fact that the risk involved in the careful operation of a carefully maintained automobile is slight, is sufficient to prevent their operation from being an ultrahazardous activity."[34] In contrast, the *Restatement* sees the airplane as an ultrahazardous activity, not exempted by the common usage proviso. Putting aside any controversy over the compulsory liability insurance feature,[35] the barrier that keeps the common law from going over to an auto compensation plan would appear to be only the issue of whether operation of autos is a matter of "common usage." There is no need here to debate the merits of the *Restatement's* formulation; our concern is simply to indicate how apparently minor an adjustment of common law liability thinking would be required to reach a compensation plan by this route. It would seem to involve no more than treating airplane and auto accidents alike. One ironic comment is in order, however. The common rhetoric on behalf of auto plans stresses the point that there are so many autos today that harm from their use has become a grave social problem requiring a special shift to strict liability. The *Restatement* stresses the same point about the number of autos to reach exactly the opposite conclusion—there are so many autos that, as a matter of common usage, auto accidents should be left to the negligence principle.

On closer analysis it appears that the argument from airplane accidents is made a bit too quickly. The *Restatement* does distinguish between airplanes and automobiles for the purpose of selecting the criterion of liability. But, at best, analogy between the two types of accident is skewed because it is only with the greatest infrequency that planes crash

---

[33] RESTATEMENT, TORTS § 520 (1938).

[34] RESTATEMENT, TORTS § 520, comment e (1938).

[35] There might, of course, be considerable controversy over the adoption of compulsory insurance. See materials in GREGORY & KALVEN, *op. cit. supra* note 2, at 733-42.

in the air. In a common sense view the salient accident problem for the auto is harm to the pedestrian or to the driver or passenger of another car, while the main accident problem for the airplane is harm to the passenger in the plane that crashes. And what is arresting for our purposes is that the *Restatement* handles the airplane's main accident problem, the airplane passenger problem, under the negligence rule and not under strict liability.[36]

The real difficulty with the approach via section 519 is that the apparently modest change required to bring the auto under strict liability turns out on further inspection to be a far-reaching move. If any distinction between ultrahazardous and ordinary risk creating activity is to be preserved, it is difficult to perceive special characteristics of auto risks that justify moving the auto across the line. If it is persuasive to see the use of the auto as ultrahazardous, it can only be because all risk creating activity is seen as ultrahazardous. To argue this is to abandon the negligence principle altogether.

We would conclude, then, that to cover the auto under strict liability would require not a small adjustment but the candid abandonment of the negligence principle for all tort situations. And the fact that at first blush it appears easy to make a small adjustment in section 519 to place the auto under strict liability is in the end evidence only of how unsatisfactory and unstable the strict liability formulation of the *Restatement* turns out to be.

The second short route to an auto compensation plan exploits a sociological perspective. The thesis is that today the overwhelming majority of cases are finally disposed of by informal settlement and not by formal trial, and that whatever the rules of liability which govern cases in court, a different set of principles seems to govern settlement practices. It is argued that the only proper way to characterize the common law system is in terms of these predominating principles. The crux of the contention is that reading backward from settlement statistics it can only be inferred that strict liability has replaced fault as the main governing criterion in the real world.

This line of argument has had a distinguished sponsorship. It was a central point of the Columbia study in the early thirties. The proponents of the Columbia plan explicitly stated that it was not necessary to debate the merits of strict liability versus fault because, in view of settlement practices, we no longer had a system based on fault; and that so far as liability was concerned, all that their proposed plan would do was to legitimate a change which had already occurred. Perhaps the most

---

[36] RESTATEMENT, TORTS § 523, comment f (1938).

vigorous statement of the thesis is that by James Landis in his review of the plan in the *Harvard Law Review:*[37]

> The committee avowedly made no inquiry as to the incidence of fault upon recovery of compensation. The figures, however, themselves demonstrate that the idea that individual moral culpability is the basis for shifting losses is little more or less than a pious fraud. Lawyers active in Massachusetts, where compulsory insurance is in force, are becoming aware that in practice the concept of negligence has given way to a working theory of absolute liability, with negligence only a factor in the measure of damages. The committee's figures illustrate that this is characteristic in any situation where the injured person seeks recovery from an insured owner or operator. The percentage of recovery, without inquiry as to fault, in insured fatal cases runs to 88%, in insured cases of permanent disability to 96%. It is hardly conceivable that the line which fault would cleave in these instances runs at all in the neighborhood of these percentages. Such figures themselves are sufficient to challenge the common law's naive assumption that fault is discoverable in the majority of automobile accidents, and yet our whole system, but for the intervention of a wisely unscientific jury, rests upon such a theory. Taught law is not tort law.

So stated, the argument has undeniable force. If it is true that the fault criterion is employed in the disposition of only a small minority of controversies, there can be no satisfactory ground for defending the retention of a negligence system. To the last generation of legal realists, this whole line of thought must have appeared as a striking breakthrough for their approach to law. But looking back, all of this seems to have been concluded too easily. As noted by Landis, no one was claiming to have compared the incidence of fault with the incidence of recovery—the fact is that no information was available regarding the incidence of fault. The conclusion that fault was inoperative as a principle rested merely on an inference from the statistics of recovery under settlements.

We now have the benefit of several recent studies. One of the most substantial comes from the on-going Columbia Project for Effective Justice.[38] In 1961 a survey was made of closing statements in all personal injury cases in New York City. For the year involved, it was estimated that 193,000 victims sought "to recover damages for injuries ascribed to

37 BOOK REVIEW, 45 HARV. L. REV. 1428-29 (1932).

38 Franklin, Chanin & Mark, *Accidents, Money and the Law: A Study of the Economics of Personal Injury Litigation*, 61 COLUM. L. REV. 1 (1961); Rosenberg & Sovern, *Delay and the Dynamics of Personal Injury Litigation*, 59 COLUM. L. REV. 1116 (1959).

someone else's fault."[39] The new Columbia study traces the history of these claims and dramatically corroborates the central findings of the 1932 study.[40] Less than 2% of the claims—a total of about 2,500—were disposed of by trial; more than 98%—a total of 190,500—were disposed of by settlement. Of the 193,000 claims, the victim recovered at least something in 84% or 162,000 instances, while in 16% or 31,000 instances there was no recovery at all.

On the basis of other information it has been estimated that 13% of all auto accident victims do not file a claim and seek recovery.[41] If we add this 13% (or some 27,000 victims) who do not file a claim and the above 16% of those who file and who are unsuccessful (some 31,000 victims), we reach a total of 58,000 victims, 27% of the total number of auto accident victims, who recover nothing. There is no way of determining in precisely how many of these cases the fault principle barred recovery, but the study itself estimated that for all claims it would be "something less than 25 per cent."[42] Moreover, of those who succeeded in obtaining recovery in New York City, which is a notably high award area, 70% got $1,000 or less, 47% got $600 or less, while 25% got $300 or less. If we put together those who recovered nothing and those who recovered $300 or less, we see that in 1961 roughly half of all the auto accident victims in New York City received $300 or less.

Interpretation of these figures requires two further qualifications. It is almost certain that a considerable number of the recoveries under $300 reflected "nuisance" settlements rather than payments made in recognition of possible liability. And where there were recoveries, whatever the level of settlement, we have no way of determining the extent to which the amount was "discounted"—that is, reduced in recognition of the risk that in litigation no liability would be found. It is wholly misleading, for example, to infer from a settlement of a $40,000 claim for $20,000, in a jurisdiction where the calendar is current, that the parties were operating on a strict liability principle; with equal plausibility it can be assumed that they got together on the assumption that in litigation there was a 50% chance of full recovery and a 50% chance of no liability.[43] What little information is available about the psychol-

---

39 Franklin, Chanin & Mark, *supra* note 38, at 10.

40 These same basic points are corroborated in James & Law, *supra* note 7. See also ZEISEL, KALVEN & BUCHHOLZ, DELAY IN THE COURT, ch. 3 (1959).

41 HUNTING & NEUWIRTH, WHO SUES IN NEW YORK CITY (1962); see also Zeisel, Book Review, N.Y.L.J., June 1962.

42 Franklin, Chanin & Mark, *supra* note 38, at 34.

43 Insofar as the settlement data came from a jurisdiction with court delay, there is also the possibility that the reduced damages reflect a "time discount," introduced by

ogy of settlements indicates that the participants in the process at least profess that they have the fault principle in mind during negotiations and that they come to terms on the basis of predictions about the odds on liability.[44]

Whatever the dominance of the settlement process, we should not lose sight altogether of the 2% of the cases that went to trial. A substantial amount of data from sources other than the Columbia Project all converge on the conclusion that when the controversy goes to litigation the defendant prevails, with a finding of no liability, about 45% of the time.[45]

A recent study, by Clarence Morris and James Paul, of the compensation of victims in auto accidents during 1946 in southeastern Pennsylvania, provides another highly useful view of the law in action.[46] In contrast to the New York estimate of 27%, the Pennsylvania study shows that some 47% of victims obtained no recovery. More important, the Pennsylvania study provides a comparison between the amounts actually received by the victims and the amounts of their medical expenses and loss of earnings—the so-called "hard" losses. It is fair to assume that in most instances where recovery is less than the amount of "hard" loss, the discount is attributable to the shadow of non-liability.[47] Using this formula we can then say that in 11% of the cases there was a discounted recovery. Putting together the 47% no recoveries and the 11% discounted awards, it is seen that something in the neighborhood of 58% of the claims may have been subject to the discipline of the liability issue. The frequency of discounted awards, moreover, rises sharply with the size of the claims. If, for example, we look only at claims for over $5,000, we can infer that in 44% of the cases the recovery was discounted.

Admittedly none of these figures is free from ambiguity.[48] But they leave no doubt that the system in operation cannot realistically be characterized as one of strict liability, even when we consider only the

---

the threat of delay. The plaintiff might settle for less in order to get his money sooner; see also ZEISEL, KALVEN & BUCHHOLZ, DELAY IN THE COURT chs. 10, 12 (1959).

[44] ZEISEL, KALVEN & BUCHHOLZ, DELAY IN THE COURT 105-09 (1959); Schneider, *Accident Litigation: The Common Man Sues*, 287 ANNALS 69, 73-74 (1953); Smithson, *Liability Claims and Litigation*, 1958 INS. L.J. 375, 381-82.

[45] For example, in the Jury Project Study of judge-jury disagreements in civil cases (see note 23 *supra*), we find for a national sample of some 4000 jury trials that the defendant does win before the jury in roughly 44% of the cases.

[46] Morris & Paul, *supra* note 11.

[47] With a qualification again, however, for the possibility of a "time discount" due to court delay; see note 43 *supra*.

[48] The study of Michigan auto accidents by Conard, which is about to be published, will hopefully put some of these ambiguities to rest; see note 12 *supra*.

cases disposed of by settlement and not by litigation. Tort law after all may be taught law.

A third short route to an auto compensation plan builds upon the implications of compulsory liability insurance statutes. We refer here to a general statute which requires liability insurance coverage as a condition to owning or operating an automobile. Such statutes are not to be confused with compensation plans since they do not and are not intended to change the basis of tort liability. Under compulsory liability insurance laws, liability for auto accidents is still keyed to negligence. Further, such measures are not to be confused with a variety of statutes extending the compulsion of insuring to a limited group of operators, as, for example, the laws regulating common carriers or the so-called financial responsibility acts.[49] Our concern is with a law which imposes the obligation to insure against liability on the entire auto owning or driving population of a state.

General compulsory insurance laws were intended to close any gaps in auto victim recovery which are due to insolvency of motorists; they were not intended to close the gaps in recovery due to the incidence of liability under the existing rules of law. Except for the insurance lobby, which has been almost heroic in the steadfastness of its opposition to these laws, there is now wide acceptance of the policy behind them.[50] The hope of easy transition from compulsory insurance to an auto compensation plan is founded on the very fact that compulsory insurance itself is now so widely acceptable. In briefest form the argument is that anyone who accepts the principle of compulsory liability insurance is no longer in a position where he can logically or even psychologically reject an auto compensation plan.[51] Two versions of the argument are made, one simple and crude, the other ingenious and tempting. Both versions rest on the perception that a compulsory insurance statute has necessarily created a massive insurance fund for paying accident victims.

The simple version argues that only a de minimis adjustment is needed to adapt such a fund to the needs of a compensation plan. Since on

[49] Grad, *Recent Developments in Automobile Accident Compensation*, 50 COLUM. L. REV. 300 (1950).

[50] EHRENZWEIG, "FULL AID" INSURANCE (1954); KLINE & PEARSON, THE PROBLEM OF THE UNINSURED MOTORIST (State of New York Insurance Department, 1951); Kalven, *Compulsory Auto Insurance?*, Chicago Sun-Times, Nov. 24, 1957, § 2, p. 3; McVay, *The Case Against Compulsory Automobile Insurance*, 15 OHIO ST. L.J. 150 (1954).

[51] As a matter of convenience in discussion, we are assuming that there will not be "under insurance" in a compulsory insurance scheme. In fact, however, the tendency of such laws is to set a low minimum for the required amount of insurance, and motorists then tend to insure only up to the minimum. Netherton, *Highway Safety Under Differing Types of Liability Legislation*, 15 OHIO ST. L.J. 110, 125 (1954); THE UNINSURED MOTORIST 3 (Virginia Ass'n of Insurance Agents, 1957).

hypothesis every auto already has insurance coverage,[52] all that the great reform requires to provide compensation to all victims is a modest adjustment upwards of insurance premiums. An initial difficulty with this approach is that the additional cost obviously will depend on the design and detail of the plan. If it turns out that only a small change in premium is required, the explanation might well be that awards under the compensation plan have been set at a radically low level. Perhaps this is a sufficient answer to the simple thesis.[53]

But what troubles and interests us in this approach is a different aspect. There is to us something odd in having the policy issue turn on what these cost magnitudes are thought to be. We sense that if the increase in annual premium were to be large, say $100, this would be taken as an argument against turning compulsory insurance into a compensation plan. And conversely if the extra premium were to be small, say $5, this would be taken as an irresistible argument for making the shift.

Under the common law it was natural to take seriously the issue of liability, for it posed the question of placing the full loss of an accident on one person or another. When the issue today is restated in insurance terms, it poses nothing more than how much the premium should be for each member of the very large community of insureds. On our view, however, the atomizing of the liability question into insurance premiums should not be permitted to cause the liability issue to evaporate. It should continue to be just as weighty an issue of policy. It is here that public law, and taxation in particular, offers a useful and needed perspective to tort law. Suppose it were proposed today to lower the personal exemption under the federal income tax from $600 to $500. Such a change, which would increase the tax by no more than $15 for most single taxpayers without dependents, would undoubtedly be regarded as raising a genuine issue of policy.[54] The concern with policy would be all the greater if it were proposed to reduce the exemption only for persons over fifty years of age. We are not passing judgment on these proposals; rather we wish to point out that those concerned with our tax system would hardly contend that the proposals raised no policy issue simply because the change in tax for any one taxpayer would be so small. Proposals to raise premiums under compulsory insurance schemes should be regarded in the same way because, given the com-

---

[52] It appears to be irrelevant for the purposes of our analysis whether we think of the insurance as "covering" the motorist or the auto.

[53] Perhaps it is not; see the discussion in section 6, *infra* pages 32 *et seq.*, of the various possibilities of reallocating damages in order to finance a plan.

[54] For taxpayers in higher rate brackets the change in exemption level would have greater dollar consequences.

pulsion by the state to insure, premium payments are close to a form of taxation. Altering the level or distribution of premiums is little different from changing the level or distribution of a tax. Hence the change from compulsory liability insurance to a compensation plan cannot be dismissed as being de minimis.

The more sophisticated version of the argument to a compensation plan from a compulsory insurance statute is not so easy to put to rest. Once the insurance fund has been created, so the argument goes, it is not the business of the insureds how the fund is distributed, so long as there is no increase in premiums and no exposure to additional liability.[55] In effect it is argued that one could devise a plan that merely would call for distributing the fund differently—that is, in accordance with strict liability rules and a reduced scale for damages. The conception is that whatever the size of the fund and whatever the demands upon it, some payments could be made to all victims without additional cost to the insureds. We are concerned here only with the single question whether the insureds have any basis for complaining about a reallocation of the fund.[56] Can this approach to a compensation plan succeed in sidestepping any of the major policy issues that are raised when it is proposed to move directly from the prevailing fault system to a compensation plan?

The question so put raises a refreshingly novel issue of policy.[57] Undoubtedly the case for a plan under this approach would have considerable political appeal since motorists could be silenced by the contention that they would be no worse off under the plan than they were before and therefore are in no position to complain. And if, as would be likely, insurance premiums were at some later day increased in order to raise awards, the motorists would then seem to have already surrendered any objection to the plan on principle. Thus the approach might appear to be an ideal strategy for moving to a compensation plan without ever confronting the underlying policy questions.

But alert motorists would find the first step to be one they could and should challenge. Again an analogy from taxation provides a guideline. We are familiar was gasoline taxes which are levied exclusively for the purpose of building and maintaining roads. Suppose the community levying such a tax decided that less money should be put into roads and more into school buildings. Would not a user of gasoline then have a

---

[55] We assume that the insurance would be sufficient to cover the liability so that payment of premiums would in effect "discharge" any potential tort liability of the insured. See discussion of "under insurance" in note 51 *supra.*

[56] Other policy issues raised by reallocating the damages fund are discussed in detail in section 6, *infra* pages 32 *et seq.*

[57] The idea we here exploit is borrowed directly from EHRENZWEIG, "FULL AID" INSURANCE (1954).

legitimate objection to holding the gasoline tax at the prevailing level in order to finance the expanded school program, even assuming that the school program is a proper use of public funds? The gasoline tax was initially justified on a benefit theory, meaning that gasoline users were financing a government operation of special benefit to them. The proposed school program cannot be made to fit into that same mold. If the road program is to be curtailed, so that less tax money is needed for its support, it would seem to follow that the gasoline tax should be trimmed accordingly. By the same token, those required to purchase liability insurance under compulsory insurance legislation are "taxed" for their premium in order to provide "benefits" to the victims of their negligence. If it is decided to modify the "expenditure" which is thus financed, and to include "benefits" to other victims, the initial theory of the "tax" would not itself support diverting for this purpose the money so collected.[58] Indeed, the analogy would call for reducing the premiums which motorists were compelled to pay. It is almost a sleight of hand to reject the fault principle in seeking to broaden the base for recoveries and yet at the same time to use the fault principle in compelling motorists to carry insurance. Once the law is liberated from fault, motorists can appropriately ask why they should pay anything.

The fourth short route to an auto compensation plan is the most familiar. It is simply to argue from the analogy to industrial accidents under workmen's compensation. In briefest form the argument is that if a compensation plan keyed to strict liability is correct policy for one great area of accidents it should be equally correct policy for another. This has been the classic analogy for proponents of compensation plans.

At this late date, only an extremely hardy soul would argue for the repeal of workmen's compensation. The question before us, therefore, is whether the basic policy issues we wish to explore for auto accidents are not already foreclosed by the decision of society, which we accept, adopting workmen's compensation.

How close is the analogy? It is worth remembering that a half century ago Jeremiah Smith confronted this issue and dramatically proclaimed that the analogy was so close that the two liability principles— that of the common law and that of workmen's compensation—were utterly and uncompromisingly contradictory.[59] Society must choose, he

---

[58] There will almost certainly be controversy as to whether the "purpose" of the tax has essentially changed. We assume in the text that there has been an essential change in purpose.

[59] Smith, *The Sequel to Workmen's Compensation Acts*, 27 HARV. L. REV. 235, 344 (1914). See also Malone, *Damage Suits and the Contagious Principle of Workmen's Compensation*, 12 LA. L. REV. 231, 234 (1952).

thundered, between the one or the other.[60] The record is now clear that Smith was not much of a prophet on this issue—society has tolerated this particular inconsistency for fifty years now. The question for us is how good an analyst he was.

We will not do more than note that there has been a curious instance of cultural lag in the conventional arguments from workmen's compensation. Workmen's compensation is being looked to as the model of a brilliant social reform at a time when, for those familiar with the field, the bloom is off the rose and there is sharp criticism of the meagerness and rigidity of award schedules, and of the costs, delays, irregularities and suspected corruption in the operation of the system.[61]

Nor will we do more than mention several differences, which some observers have urged as critical, between the industrial accident situation and the auto accident situation. It is said that while the industrial accident is relatively fixed and easy to investigate, the auto accident is more transient and difficult to investigate. The result is that there are likely to be great differences in the opportunities for policing fraudulent claims in the two areas.[62] It is also said that damages are more amenable to scheduling in the one case than in the other, both because the range and variety of physical injuries is more restricted in the industrial accident, and because the injured personnel are drawn from a fairly homogeneous economic group.[63] These are acute observations, and they do point up specific difficulties which would be encountered in administering a compensation plan, but they do not cut deep enough to put to rest Jeremiah Smith's challenge of fundamental inconsistency.

There are three residual differences which lead us to deny the analogy to workmen's compensation. First, there is a great difference between the common law system for industrial accidents which workmen's compensation was created to replace and the common law system for auto accidents which exists today. Under the law of fifty years ago, we are told, the ability of the injured employee to recover was greatly circumscribed by the well-known trilogy of employer defenses—assumption of risk, con-

[60] "Without indicating our own view as to the intrinsic justice, either of the Workmen's Compensation Legislation or of the common law of A.D. 1900, it seems safe to say that the basic principles of the two are irreconcilable. They cannot both be wholly right, or both wholly wrong." Smith, *supra* note 59, at 368.

[61] Compare Riesenfeld, *Basic Problems in the Administration of Workmen's Compensation*, 36 MINN. L. REV. 119 (1952).

[62] Lilly, *Compensation for Automobile Accidents: A Symposium*, 32 COLUM. L. REV. 803 (1932); Monaghan, *The Liability Claim Racket*, 3 LAW & CONTEMP. PROB. 491 (1936).

[63] Brown, *Automobile Accident Litigation in Wisconsin: A Factual Study*, 10 WIS. L. REV. 170 (1934).

tributary negligence, and the fellow servant rule. The old law has looked to some like a conspiracy to throw the losses of industrial accidents onto employees as a class at a time when they were conspicuously less well off than their employers. There is no comparable harshness in the law which confronts the auto accident claimant today. In the same vein, the whole "welfare" support for workmen's compensation is considerably diluted today in the auto accident area. First party insurance and social legislation have come on the scene and have greatly reduced the likelihood that the auto accident victim and his family will bear the full brunt of the accident.

A second difference is that the enterprise situation made possible a popular myth as to how the cost of workmen's compensation was to be borne. The widespread image was that by placing the cost of workmen's compensation on employers the cost would be passed on to consumers of their products through operation of market forces. The result was thought to be that not only social justice but economic justice would be accomplished; and this view of the matter was crystallized in the slogan that the cost of products should reflect the blood of workmen. Although there are good reasons today for doubting whether consumers do bear the cost of workmen's compensation,[64] for our immediate purposes it is enough that there is no one in the auto situation who occupies a role which the employer was popularly thought to play in the industrial accident situation—no one, that is, who could be regarded as being in a position to pass on the costs to consumers via the market.

A third difference challenges the view that workmen's compensation offers a competing doctrine of tort liability. There is no doubt that this is the traditional view; workmen's compensation was enacted to repeal and replace common law tort rules, and it was challenged and ratified in court on that premise.[65] We wish to suggest here a considerably different view of the history and rationale. In retrospect, we are impressed that workmen's compensation can best be understood as a kind of "fringe benefit" incorporated by law into the basic employment contract. The law in effect compelled the employer to provide, as a term of employment, an industrial accident policy for his employees.

Several strands of thought support this perspective. In his highly regarded casebook on Agency, Roscoe Steffen groups materials so as to place workmen's compensation as part of the employment relationship.[66] He suggests that the legal history of personal injuries to employees could

64 H. G. Brown, The Economics of Taxation, ch. 6 (1924).

65 New York Central R.R. v. White, 243 U.S. 188 (1916); Ives v. South Buffalo Ry., 201 N.Y. 201, 94 N.E. 431 (1911).

66 Steffen, Cases on Agency §§ 9-10 (2d ed. 1952).

easily have been different—that courts could readily have handled the whole problem as an aspect of the employee's indemnity action against the employer for losses incurred in the course of an agency relationship.[67] There is a contemporary analogue in the tendency today to use workmen's compensation as a base, and through collective bargaining to expand the benefits to cover unemployment, sickness and accidents off work.[68] What we wish to emphasize is that this continuum from statutory benefits to collective bargaining agreements can be read backwards, so as to view the whole as part of the employer-employee contract. The distinctive quality is that each of these forms of coverage is tied in to the employment nexus. On this view the issue to which workmen's compensation is addressed is primarily that of determining the terms and conditions of employment.

In stressing this somewhat novel rationale for workmen's compensation, our chief purpose has been to point up a significant difference between the industrial accident and the auto accident. Unlike workmen's compensation, there is no contractual nexus on which auto compensation plans can build.

Thus we conclude that the reason society has for so long tolerated different legal principles for industrial accidents and for the tort field generally is that, Jeremiah Smith to the contrary, the two areas are essentially different.

4

In the discussion of auto compensation, it is generally assumed that the state will have to intervene with its coercive powers to effectuate the plan. But in the last fifteen years, the possibility of a voluntary plan has drawn increased attention. It will be convenient for us to indulge in one more analytic detour before proceeding to discuss compensation plans on their merits, and to ask whether society can arrive at a plan through wholly voluntary action. It goes without saying that the policy questions disappear if voluntary action produces a plan.

In an article in 1948, Fleming James reviewed the major developments in the automobile liability insurance policy, such as the omnibus clause and the medical payments clause, and concluded that a revolution in

---

[67] "The transition, all within less than a century, from an individualistic economy engaged in petty trade to the present highly specialized industrial system made it necessary for the courts to formulate much new 'law.' Ready at hand was the indemnity pattern already marked out to cover the agents' pecuniary risks." *Id.* at 146-47. See D'Arcy v. Lyle, 5 Binn. 441 (Pa. 1813). Compare MALONE & PLANT, CASES ON WORKMEN'S COMPENSATION x (1963).

[68] Katz & Wirpel, *Workmen's Compensation 1910-1950: Are Present Benefits Adequate?*, 4 LAB. L.J. 167 (1953); Larson, *The Future of Workmen's Compensation*, 6 NACCA L.J. 18 (1950).

auto accident compensation was being quietly accomplished through contract on the initiative of insurance companies.[69] About a decade ago, Albert Ehrenzweig, building on the medical payments or first-aid clause, proposed a scheme of what he called Full Aid Insurance, which he claimed yielded a voluntary compensation plan.[70] And a year or so ago, Robert A. Rennie, an insurance executive, saw in the modern family compensation coverage provision the germ of a fully developed compensation plan.[71] Thus the idea of a plan through voluntary contract is certainly in the air.

The common denominator here is that the auto owner voluntarily insures beyond his liability. In the case of the omnibus clause, the owner is in effect buying liability coverage for one who drives his car with his consent but for whose negligence in many instances he would not be liable. In the case of the medical payments clause the owner is in effect buying accident insurance for occupants of his car for whose injuries he again in many instances might not be liable. The broad vision is that since owners will go this far voluntarily, they might be persuaded to go farther and buy accident coverage for anyone injured by their car regardless of liability. If so, the result would be the functional equivalent of a compensation plan and would have been arrived at voluntarily.

The recent development of the so-called family compensation coverage in liability policies comes closest to this vision. Under the coverage, the insured, his passengers, and third party claimants are given the option of accepting payment under a schedule contained in the policy in lieu of resorting to their common law remedy. The current schedule in one such policy has been described as follows: "[I]t provides immediate benefits with limits of $2,900 in case of injury and $7,900 in case of death for each person regardless of fault. These benefits cover medical expenses up to $2,000 for each injured person. In addition, there are disability indemnity benefits at $5 per day for 180 days plus a death benefit of $5,000 per person."[72]

The earlier forms of meta-liability insurance, such as the omnibus clause, suggested strongly the idea of Good Samaritan insurance tempered by the social utility of doing a favor for one to whom you were lending your car. It is obvious that so long as people are willing to make gifts to others through insurance coverage, there is no limit to the extension of coverage by voluntary contract. The family compensation schedule

---

[69] James, *Accident Liability Reconsidered: The Impact of Liability Insurance*, 57 YALE L.J. 549 (1948).

[70] Ehrenzweig, "FULL AID" INSURANCE (1954).

[71] Rennie, *An Experiment in Limited Absolute Liability*, 29 J. INS. 177 (1963).

[72] *Id.* at 179-80.

brings in another theme. The provision is in effect simply a firm offer of settlement from the insurance company. The motivation for it is the desire to speed up the settlement process, to eliminate lawyer interference, and to effect economies in the company's handling of claims. Again, it is obvious that so long as the injured are willing to settle on the scheduled terms, there is no limit to the extension of recovery by voluntary contract. The crucial question is, therefore, how far this strategy of voluntary contract can move us toward providing satisfactory compensation for all accident victims.

The data reported for the early years of experience under the family compensation provision are illuminating; they make it abundantly clear that there is no magic in these matters and that the expected sources of resistance will be stubborn indeed.

The provision was sold in two ways: with an explicit charge for the additional coverage and with an arrangement for remittance of premium for those who did not choose the additional coverage. The extra premium cost was roughly $6 to $7 a year. Under the remittance scheme, where affirmative action was required *to avoid* the new coverage, some 66% of the insureds accepted the coverage. However, under the separate charge arrangement, where affirmative action was required *to obtain* the coverage, only 33% of insureds did so.[73] This suggests the central difficulty with all such proposals: They must rely on the charity of the insured, if he understands what he is being asked to buy, and few people are likely to be very charitable. In brief, Good Samaritan insurance will appeal largely to Good Samaritans.

Another aspect of the reported data concerns the kinds of claims on which the offer of settlement was accepted. Two strong impressions emerge. One is that statistically the very small claims dominate: thus 63% of all payments to third parties under the schedule were less than $50, 79% were less than $100, and 90% were less than $200. The other impression is that in the occasional case of a substantial payment under the schedule, the claimant is unlikely to have qualified for recovery under common law. The suspicions these figures tend to confirm are that a strict liability offer of settlement of this sort is likely to recruit largely the nuisance claims and the clear no-liability cases, and that it likely will leave largely untouched the main business of the common law torts system today.[74]

[73] *Id.* at 181.

[74] It thus functions somewhat perversely as a plan, tending to give prompt recovery to what at common law were the weaker claims. Further, it is unlikely to provide a remedy for court congestion by affecting the settlement ratio. See ZEISEL, KALVEN & BUCHHOLZ, DELAY IN THE COURT, 108 n.5 (1959).

These two inescapable difficulties of voluntary coverage can be ex‑ pected to reinforce each other. As the generosity of the settlement offer is increased in order to extend its effectiveness, the cost of the provision to the insured will also increase. And as that cost rises, the attractiveness of the provision to the insured will diminish. In the end, the main promise for a voluntary plan, except as it conceals from insureds the cost of such extended coverage, is the undertaking of the insurance com‑ panies to procure and disburse the gifts made by the insureds—and nothing more.

We thus conclude that only a very limited approach to a plan can be made through the voluntary route, and that to reach a full scale plan the coercion of the state is required. And we would observe further that the reluctance of motorists to make charitable contributions to a fund for accident victims underscores the importance of finding a sound and convincing basis for employing the powers of the state to compel the contributions.

5

We have devoted our efforts thus far to salvaging the issues we now wish to confront. On our view we have established that fault is a suffi‑ ciently feasible criterion of liability so that the current system cannot be said to fall of its own weight; that the current system in actual opera‑ tion, particularly in the context of liability insurance and the settlement practices of insurance companies, does not so closely approach a de facto compensation scheme that we are simply being asked to legitimate a change that has already occurred; and that no combination of voluntary action is likely to produce a compensation plan. To change from the common law system to a compensation plan will make a real difference. We now wish to explore the merits of using state power to effectuate such a change.

As we noted at the outset, one main objective of compensation plans is the elimination of any gaps in coverage due not to liability rules but to insolvency of motorists. For this purpose, plans rely on creating a fund through compulsory insurance or the taxing power, out of which claims are to be paid.[75] Although all plans have this underwriting element, it is not a distinctive characteristic. Nothing prevents the common law from using compulsory liability insurance.

But all compensation plans do have two common characteristics which mark their key differences from the common law. The distinctive feature of the common law is that it does not intend that all victims of accidents recover; it leaves the loss where it falls for certain categories of victims—

---

[75] If the taxing power is used, there need not be, in a literal sense, a fund built up.

the single car accident victim, the negligent victim, and the victim in an accident where the other party was not negligent. The liability pattern and hence the criteria as to when compensation will be paid are deliberately complex. As a consequence, there frequently is controversy over the merits of particular claims and delay in paying claims destined ultimately to be paid.

All compensation plans have as their two main targets the elimination of some or all the gaps in common law coverage and a drastic improvement in the timing of payment to victims.[76] These two objectives are necessarily interrelated. The improvement in timing of awards depends on extension of coverage. Acceleration of payment to victims rests largely on simplifying the liability criteria, and this in turn rests in large part on extending the coverage of victims so as to hold to a minimum the job of distinguishing between good and bad claims. A proper appraisal of the merits of plans calls for looking at both the coverage issue and the timing issue. Since on our view the coverage issue is the more basic, our agenda for discussion will be first to examine at length extension of coverage and only then to turn to improvement in the timing of compensation.

To accomplish the extension of coverage, a plan must change the allocation of costs generally. Stated simply, the money for the newly covered victims must come from somewhere. There have been various suggestions as to where the money should come from, and it is these that for us mark the most important differences among the plans. A recurrent image, derived from thinking in common law liability categories, is that the only possibility is to put the cost of additional coverage on motorists. It is important to stress that there are three major alternatives. One is to put none of the cost of additional coverage on motorists, but to redistribute losses among victims through changing the rules as to damages, thus in effect placing the cost of the additional coverage on some victims. Another possibility is to take all the costs off actual victims and to place the cost of all accidents on all potential victims, thereby putting the costs of accidents on society as a whole rather than on some identifiable group in society. Still another possibility is to finance the additional coverage out of the economies of administration expected to be derived from moving to a plan. We might note in passing that most, if not all, plans pro-

---

[76] There may also be the advantage of "pacing" payments to the victims so as to reduce the danger of his squandering a large capital sum. It is another characteristic of the common law that it takes no interest in what happens to damages once they are paid in a lump sum to the plaintiff. Occasionally, in a creative settlement, the money has been put into a trust fund. See James, *The Columbia Study of Compensation for Automobile Accidents: An Unanswered Challenge*, 59 COLUM. L. REV. 408, 412 (1959).

posed to date are hybrids which have drawn on a combination of two or more of these possibilities.

From the beginning the common law has had the simple view that when a loss was shifted it could only be shifted from one individual to another; and when liability insurance came along it was seen officially only as a device for guaranteeing the solvency of parties onto whom a loss might be shifted.[77] The right of a plaintiff to compensation was necessarily paralleled by the duty of a defendant to compensate him. Therefore the cost issue as such did not arise but was handled automatically through disposition of the liability issue. By way of contrast, under plans the compensation question is divorced from the cost question. If the loss is to be shifted, it is viewed as being shifted from the individual victim to a compensation fund. And, correlatively, the duty to contribute to a fund for accident victims is thought of as having only the faintest resemblance to common law liability for negligent conduct.

We have now reached a point where we can put our own position affirmatively. If the additional coverage sought by a plan could be accomplished without cost to anyone, there of course would be no argument against obtaining something for nothing. But so long as there is a cost which must somehow be borne, we have not succeeded in escaping the original tough policy question of the common law: What is the fair way of allocating the cost of losses from auto accidents? The affirmative issues we wish to discuss are presented by the choices available among the alternative avenues for distributing the cost of additional loss shifting.

6

One major alternative for shifting losses under compensation plans is to hold constant the costs to motorists and to obtain money for the desired additional coverage by changing the pattern in which the compensation fund is distributed among victims. To develop this alternative all we need is the simple idea that one way of finding money to cover new victims is to give less to victims already compensable under common law.

We are not unmindful that in exploring short cuts to plans we touched on the strategy of reaching a plan by redistributing the fund from which damages are to be paid.[78] It will be helpful to summarize here the thrust of our prior discussion. In brief we do not find persuasive the contention that a plan will be costless because the reduction in damage awards can be made large enough to defray the cost of covering addi-

---

77 Laube, *The Social Vice of Accident Indemnity*, 80 U. Pa. L. Rev. 189 (1931).
78 See section 3, *supra* pages 15 *et seq.*

tional victims. Our view is that if such reductions are effectuated, the benefits in justice belong to the motorists insured. To divert the benefits to new victims, through a plan, is no more plausible to us than to give them to charity.

Nevertheless, we recognize that there is great political appeal to the strategy of appearing to hold costs constant by financing additional coverage through rearranging the pattern of damage awards. We are also aware that for half a century it has been characteristic of plans to propose that part of the loss be borne by victims[79]—indeed, workmen's compensation was ratified constitutionally on the basis of a legislative bargain under which the employer was seen as trading his liability advantages at common law for a limitation on damages.[80] It will be worthwhile, therefore, to explore the implications of this alternative for shifting losses, without prejudicing our underlying objection to financing a plan by juggling damage levels.

The focus of discussion now changes from criticisms of common law liability theory to consideration of common law damages theory. Emancipated for the moment from the common law idea of awarding full compensation for personal injury due to the fault of another, we reach the not often asked question: What other criteria might there be for determining how to distribute a compensation fund among accident victims? Several deserve exploration.

The common law damage system has two hallmarks: damages are tailored to the individual case, and the damage principle, whatever its imperfections relating to fees and interest, looks to awarding full compensation to victims.[81] It follows that there are two basic courses for changing the common law. The principle of individualized damages could be given up and damages computed on the basis of a schedule, or the level of awards could be lowered.

To aid in analysis here we will begin by exercising the academic prerogative of proposing a model that is most unlikely to find supporters in the real world. The simplest approach to financing coverage for additional victims by reducing the level of damages would be to treat the fund, created by insurance, as though it were the assets of a bankrupt's estate and to provide for some variety of pro-rata distribution among

---

[79] This was, for example, a principal point in the original Ballentine proposal. Ballentine, *A Compensation Plan for Railway Accident Claims*, 29 HARV. L. REV. 705 (1916).

[80] See note 65 *supra*.

[81] Kalven, *The Jury, the Law, and the Personal Injury Damage Award*, 19 OHIO ST. L.J. 158 (1958). This remains true under comparative negligence. Damages are measured under a full compensation principle even though there is a discount for plaintiff's own faulty contribution to the damages.

victims. This might even be done literally by retaining the common law criteria of damages in order to get a base figure for each victim which then could be scaled down by an appropriate fraction. For example, if the additional coverage doubled the number of claimants, each would receive one-half the damages as measured by common law standards. Under this model there would be several striking results: All victims would get some recovery; all victims who would have been compensable at common law would be worse off under the plan; all victims would bear part of their loss themselves without shifting it; all victims would bear their loss in the same ratio; and the extent to which losses were compensated under the scheme would depend merely on how much was in the fund and how many victims there were to share it—and thus the new coverage could be financed regardless of what its cost turned out to be.

However rough, this model has the merit of raising sharply two issues basic to all proposals to reallocate damages. If the common law assessment of damages is thought to be correct, then any reduction will represent a real loss to the hitherto eligible victims. We are then confronted with the question of what the offsetting gain from increased coverage is. The answer is quite interesting: The gain in coverage can only inure to the benefit of those hitherto ineligible for recovery, and this means the single car accident victim, the negligent victim, and the victim of the non-negligent driver. We thus reach an issue that has considerable bite —whether we should shift awards away from "deserving victims" in order to compensate "less deserving victims."[82] Further, if the plan is to leave some of the loss where it falls, why should it not leave all of it there? One answer undoubtedly would be that such a model offers a prudent way of splitting losses between actors and victims. This rejoinder, however, is not persuasive; the common law itself might well be viewed as a system that also splits losses between actors and victims. And the common law solution of vertical splitting—full recoveries in some cases and no recoveries in others—might well have more appeal than the new proposal for horizontal splitting—partial recoveries in all cases.

A second model for damages, which also calls for retaining the common law principle of individualized damages, would finance the coverage of additional victims by restricting compensation to so-called "realistic" losses. The underlying thought is that the common law now over-com-

---

82 The adjective "less deserving" is a bit unfair. The majority of the beneficiaries will be those who would have been barred by contributory negligence at common law; however, the other beneficiaries will be the victims of single car accidents and the victims in accidents where there was no negligence on the part of any driver.

pensates victims by awarding damages for pain and suffering. This approach to financing a plan is responsive to a widely-voiced criticism of the common law system of damages—a criticism which often is made independently of any concern with compensation plans.[83]

While it is fashionable today to talk of eliminating pain and suffering as a luxury item of damages, and while it is true also that workmen's compensation has made a successful stab at this for over a generation, the case for compensating pain and suffering is not without strength. The whole idea of pain and suffering is usually taken too literally by its critics, as though it were a third specific heading of damages which the jury or judge adds on to medical expense and economic loss in computing the total damages. The University of Chicago Law School's Jury Project has developed data which suggests that the process of pricing injuries is far more fluid: It is much more a search for a felt appropriate sum for the particular injury than it is a problem of addition.[84] If pain and suffering were ruled out in instructing juries, damage awards by juries might well be as high as they are now. The jury seems to be responding not to pain as such but to the dignitary aspects of the injury, and these can be considerable in cases where there is no pain. It is not merely sentimentality of the jury that is at work. Consider the case of the man who loses a leg in an accident; assume he makes a rapid successful adjustment, gets his job back and suffers no current pain.[85] What is at stake in the debate over pain and suffering is whether the law is to treat him as entitled only to compensation for his medical expense plus temporary loss of income, or whether it is to try to translate into monetary terms the gross indignity he has suffered, which has surely altered his entire life. To pursue seriously the removal of pain and suffering leads quickly to the more challenging issue of eliminating all compensation for dignitary harm. And this is especially true when we remember that auto accident redress, unlike workmen's compensation, must cover a wide and heterogeneous army of claimants. The typical workmen's compensation plaintiff is a wage earner within a fairly narrow age range and even narrower salary range; it is plausible to think of his loss as measured by loss of wages. A substantial number of auto accident victims are in other categories: the very young child whose economic loss cannot even be conjectured, the housewife who has never previously earned money, the re-

83 Jaffe, *Damages for Personal Injury: The Impact of Insurance,* 18 LAW & CONTEMP. PROB. 219 (1953); Morris, *Liability for Pain and Suffering,* 59 COLUM. L. REV. 476 (1959); Plant, *Damages for Pain and Suffering,* 19 OHIO ST. L.J. 200 (1958).

84 Kalven, *supra* note 81.

85 Compare McNulty v. Southern Pacific Co., 96 Cal. App. 2d 841, 216 P.2d 534 (1950).

tired person living off an annuity, and so on. In these cases the economic loss is impossible to locate and unless damages are to be limited to medical expenses, some recognition of dignitary losses must be left in the system.[86]

As we look at other damage models for financing plans, it is noteworthy that all turn away from the common law principle of individualized damages and utilize a schedule of awards. Presumably this reflects a wish to reduce the areas of controversy and to simplify procedures for recovering compensation.

Analytically, the concept of a damage schedule might itself be viewed as a third model which involves nothing more than striking averages for categories of claims. On initial impression, scheduling would appear to be neutral as to the level of damages—the schedule averages could in theory be set at any level desired. But on further reflection it appears that the use of scheduling almost invariably will result in lowering the level of damages. The explanation lies in the problem of handling dignitary harm. A decision to include a significant dignitary component makes the scheduling of damages a complex task. Let us return again to our victim who has lost a leg and consider the problem of scheduling appropriate damages which will reflect the indignity to him. How many distinctions would we wish to recognize? The difference between men and women? Between adults and children? Between old and young? Urban and rural? Athletic and sedentary? As we spin out these questions, we become aware that in scheduling, one tends to decide against giving any substantial weight to dignitary harm, without really confronting the underlying policy issue. It is doubtful whether, compensation plans apart, anyone would urge making this change in damage law for its own sake.

Through scheduling we can develop a fourth and fifth model for compensating victims which are more radical and more imaginative departures from the common law damage pattern. Our fourth model would borrow directly from social insurance norms. The thesis is that the legal system should provide not full compensation but, as with other welfare measures, compensation at a minimum satisfactory subsistence level.[87] Whereas the common law would seek to give the victim enough to bring him back to whatever level he had been at before the accident, this model

---

[86] Compare the policy argument urged in one of the earliest cases giving an explicit justification for awarding damages for pain and suffering, Morse v. Auburn & Syracuse R.R., 10 N.Y. 621 (1851).

[87] For present purposes, we happily do not need a precise definition of this ambiguous and controversial standard.

would seek to give the victim only enough to cure the social disaster of the injury.[88]

At first thought the idea of treating the tort system as performing the social welfare service of taking care of the needy seems full of promise, but on reflection serious strains are disclosed. We must emphasize that if we are to talk the idiom of social welfare we must be willing to accept the consequence that the problem is then to be analyzed in a social welfare framework and that this framework raises issues quite different from those customary in tort law.

Any such approach must confront a difficulty common to all social insurance proposals: In deciding on compensation for victims, are we to look at the actual economic position of the individual victim, considering his own income and wealth and the other resources society makes available to him? If the answer is yes, we presumably will decide not to compensate from our fund those victims who are relatively well off or who have adequate insurance protection from other sources. If the answer is no, there is the old paradox of paying under a relief rationale some victims who are not in need.

A more serious shortcoming is that such a welfare scheme confined within the limits of the auto accident problem becomes absurdly ad hoc, from the viewpoint both of the victims and of financing the plan. As to the victims, it would involve singling out from the universe of the needy those persons who happen to be in auto accidents. The needy man who falls crossing the street, to say nothing of the needy man who suffers from disabling disease, would not be a beneficiary or concern of the fund.

When we turn to the sources of financing for the welfare fund, the picture becomes still more odd. The general logic we are pursuing here is to assume that any additional coverage will be financed by a reallocation of damage awards among victims. In the subsistence model under discussion, this means that payments for the needy victims of auto accidents would, in effect, be contributed by the victims of auto accidents who would have had good claims under the common law and who are not in need. The full artificiality of this reallocation is realized if we think of financing the same welfare goals via taxation. Who would ever propose taxing well-to-do victims of auto accidents in order to make welfare payments to that fraction of the needy who happen to be victims of auto accidents?

We can now voice the suspicion that the social problem of the victim, which has generated the momentum for this model, is really the age old

---

[88] Compare the Mexican death damage scheme described by Justice Holmes in Slater v. Mexican National R.R., 194 U.S. 120 (1904).

problem of poverty. The victim's claim to the government's attention rests on being a needy case. If we were to make the magical assumption that overnight the lower third in the wealth and income scale in our society was brought substantially above a satisfactory subsistence level, how much appeal would such a compensation plan have?[89]

In any event, the subsistence approach highlights how fascinatingly different the rationale of the common law really is. Under the common law the victims recover as a matter of right (because they were wronged) and not as a case for public charity or assistance. Perhaps this is why no one finds it congenial to argue for minimum subsistence compensation to eligible victims under a fault system, or conversely to argue for full compensation to all victims under a compensation plan. The common law commitment to fault and to full compensation seem to go hand in hand.

A fifth and last damage model is in effect the inverse of that just discussed. Applying the principle of major medical expense insurance,[90] this model would leave all losses on victims up to a specified level; beyond that level it would provide scheduled compensation for all auto accident victims. The rationale for such an approach is that individuals might be expected to absorb small losses without catastrophic consequences and that a serious social problem emerges only when the loss is substantial. The fund would be available to deal only with the serious social problems; but to avoid administrative difficulties, the system might ignore other means at the disposal of the victims.

Instead of treating the uncompensated victims as an undifferentiated mass, this approach, recently explored by Clarence Morris and James Paul,[91] seeks to focus on that aspect of the problem which is of greatest concern to society. The approach, like the minimum subsistence model, is sharply different from the common law in that the victim does not claim as a matter of right (because he was wronged), but rather as a case of a social problem. For the common law it is a matter of justice between individuals; for both of these alternatives to the common law, it is a matter of a proper solution to a social problem involving the relationship between the victim and the state. The difference between the minimum subsistence model and the major medical expense model

---

[89] But the magic of the example may be unfair. The fact that poverty may be viewed as a relative matter does not make it any less painful for those who experience it.

[90] Although there are comparable provisions in many accident insurance policies today, we use this "nickname" because the major medical arrangement is more widely known.

[91] Morris & Paul, *The Financial Impact of Automobile Accidents*, 110 U. PA. L. REV. 913 (1962).

is that the former sees the serious social problem as that of poverty, while the latter sees it as that of a sudden catastrophe. On our view, both social problems undoubtedly are serious to some extent today, but as society grows more prosperous, the catastrophe element is likely to become relatively more significant and demanding than the poverty component. Moreover, the major medical expense model appears to be the more appropriate one for dealing specifically with the automobile accident problem. As we have pointed out, poverty is a general problem of which the automobile accident is only a minor part; and for that reason, if for no other, a compensation plan is not a particularly appropriate vehicle for dealing with poverty. In contrast, the major medical expense model can be geared to dealing with extraordinary expenses or costs arising in defined circumstances, and thus could be tailored to fit the automobile accident situation. Not the least virtue of the major medical model is that it allows for considerable flexibility in setting the level of the threshold at which loss is shifted off the victims. Quite likely, the deductible amount could be set high enough, without doing violence to the rationale, to cover all victims and not put additional costs on motorists. Such a model is ideal for dramatizing the issues for policy debate.

It can now be seen that these various damage models have an interesting relationship to each other. Each, in contrast to the common law, would finance new coverage by leaving part of the loss with the otherwise compensable victims. The bankruptcy model would leave a constant fraction of the total loss on each victim; the "realistic damages" model would leave the pain and suffering component of his loss fully on each victim; the subsistence model would leave all of the loss above a minimum subsistence recovery level on the victim; the major medical expense model would leave all the loss below a specified threshold level on the victim. Further, each of these models operates on a different assumption as to the function of compensation awards. The bankruptcy model builds on the assumption that the size of the fund is controlling and that the size of the fund depends on considerations which are independent of the aggregate losses of the victims. The "realistic damages" model builds on the assumption that all real losses, but only real losses, should be compensated and that pain and suffering is not a real loss. The minimum subsistence model builds on the assumption that the urgent function of compensation is to prevent people from falling below a subsistence level as a result of an auto accident. The major medical model builds on the assumption that the urgent function of compensation is to cover the catastrophic impact of the individual accident. Finally, all these models are in contrast to the common law. Under it only some victims are eligible for awards; all eligible victims are entitled to be made whole regardless of the total costs; being made whole includes a decent recognition of pain and suffering; and damages are to be computed individually for each case.

We thus reach the end of our exploration of the alternatives for financing the additional coverage required by a plan through reallocating awards. Constructing possible models is a useful exercise in that it serves to locate refreshing questions about the theory and function of compensation. But the reallocation of damages as a method for financing a plan remains unpersuasive. The case for it stumbles over two difficulties. First, if the general level of damages is to be reduced, we have yet to find sufficient reason for giving the benefits of the reduction to newly covered victims instead of to motorist insureds. Second, if the total fund contributed by motorists is to remain constant, we have yet to see why the old victims should be forced to share it with the new victims.

7

A second major alternative for meeting the costs of additional coverage under a compensation plan is to posit an arrangement under which the potential victims insure themselves against injury regardless of third party fault. In theory damages could be measured as at common law; but to avoid any distractions which may come from being so unrealistic, we will assume that damages are to be fixed by schedule. By carrying such insurance, the victims create a fund which would be available to cover their losses. This arrangement would achieve the objective of shifting the loss off the immediate victim. All victims would be covered under it and they would shift their losses to the insurance fund.

It will be readily perceived that there are at least three lines of objection to this scheme. The first becomes evident when we translate it back into common law terms. In effect, the scheme would be tantamount to the abolition of all common law liability for auto accidents and substitution of a plan of compulsory accident insurance for victims. The objection then goes to the old point that no one should be compelled to pay premiums to insure against losses caused by the fault of another.[92] While we find this to be a congenial argument against the arrangement offered, it need not detain us because the other objections are much more powerful. A second line of objection derives from the traditional presumption against sumptuary legislation. Everyone is already at liberty to spend his resources for auto accident insurance, but it is difficult to see why the state should intervene and compel him to do so. Although

[92] See the discussion of recovery over in section 13 *infra* at page 84.

we would not reject out of hand all sumptuary legislation, we do urge that there is some merit in calling a spade a spade. It is at this place that an infrequently noticed detail of the Columbia plan becomes striking. The draftsmen explicitly considered and rejected the desirability of having their proposed compensation fund cover injuries in single car accidents. Since there was agreement that a driver should always be covered if he crashed into another car, it seemed odd not to protect him where he crashed into a tree. The draftsmen nevertheless decided that inclusion of the single car accident would change the basic rationale of the plan and would raise serious constitutional doubts about it.[93] They recognized that such an extension of the plan would in effect call for compelling each operator of an auto to insure himself against damage in an accident in which no other auto operator was involved. The heart of the matter was that it seemed anomalous to prevent a person from driving unless he insured himself against damages he might sustain from smashing into a tree. We call attention to the puzzle whether the single car accident should be covered by a plan because it highlights the awkwardness of creating a compensation fund that forces victims to insure themselves.

A third line of objection to our first party insurance model is the least theoretical and most decisive. It has often been observed that proponents of plans usually rely on financing a compensation fund through use of liability insurance, and there has been a call to be more imaginative about the use of insurance. However, it is not habit alone which keeps the plans tied to liability insurance. The main (if not only) alternative to liability insurance is accident insurance, and the difficulty in using it is very basic: There is no practical way of enforcing a system of compulsory auto accident insurance. Everyone in the society is a potential auto accident victim and therefore the usual arrangement of making insurance a license prerequisite is not available. Moreover, even if some way could be found to solve the enforcement problem, the administrative costs of selling insurance to the entire population would be prohibitive. It would be uneconomic in the extreme to single out accidents from so narrow a source and require that that risk alone be covered by a separate insurance policy for each person or family unit.

These practical difficulties suggest that if compulsory accident insurance is thought desirable, a mechanism akin to taxation must be utilized to collect the premiums. We thus come to the major alternative of social insurance.

---

[93] Dowling, *Compensation for Automobile Accidents: A Symposium*, 32 COLUM. L. REV. 813 (1932); Lewis, *The Merits of the Automobile Accident Compensation Plan*, 3 LAW & CONTEMP. PROB. 583, 592 (1936).

A feasible way of exploiting the social insurance alternative would be to extend in some way the existing welfare legislation system to cover auto accident injuries. It can be assumed for purposes of analysis that this is done either at the state or the federal level.[94] It can also be assumed for the present that the extension is to be financed by what is virtually a flat tax on covered individuals, without contribution by employers and without any contribution out of general tax revenues.[95] What we would have then is compulsory accident insurance financed by "premiums" collected from the insureds by the government through its tax mechanism.

The compelling analogy now comes from another quarter. Traditionally, compensation plans are treated as evolving from the common law liability system; they are viewed as building upward from the common law. The social security arrangement makes it readily apparent that we can begin in a wholly different part of the legal map and come down to the auto accident problem. The post-war development in England is nicely illustrative.[96] In 1947 the *Beveridge Report*, based on the broadest possible welfare rationale, recommended adoption of social insurance covering medical care and unemployment. At almost the last minute tort law was remembered, and the question then arose whether there was any point in keeping the tort law alive in view of the new social insurance scheme. In typical English fashion, the conflict was not squarely resolved but rather a compromise was adopted under which some fraction of the social insurance benefits was to be deducted from common law damages. What is important in this story for our purposes is that it shows how easy it is to solve the auto accident problem without thinking about it specifically. From the perspective of social insurance, the auto accident problem is just one among many details of the total welfare issue.

The merits of solving the auto accident problem through social security cannot be appraised within the provincial borders of the traditional tort viewpoint; they must be considered in the same terms as any other extension of social security or welfare coverage. Every increase in social insurance restricts the individual's freedom of choice in consumption. At some level of social insurance coverage, any further limitation on the individual surely must outweigh the gain from the increased insurance protection. And at any level of social insurance coverage, a choice must be made among the alternative types of coverage which can be compar-

---

94 The federalism aspect might pose a severe practical problem, but it is beyond the special concerns of this essay.

95 See note 94 *supra;* a comparable comment applies here.

96 Friedman, *Social Insurance and the Principles of Tort Liability*, 63 HARV. L. REV. 241 (1949).

ably financed. In this context, auto accident injuries would compete with illness, disease and misfortunes from other sources. The fact that the state is already heavily involved in the administration of compensation for auto accident injuries should not of itself give auto injuries a preferred position in that competition. We find unpersuasive the argument that the auto accident is to be preferred to cancer as an object for state welfare intervention simply because, due to the development of the common law liability system, the state is already intervening in the one case and not the other.[97]

Nonetheless, the social security alternative is good enough to serve as a challenge against which to measure any other proposed compensation plan. The question it puts before the house is: If another plan is thought to be good, why isn't the social security arrangement better?

Before leaving the compulsory accident insurance alternative, we must deal with one other point which arguably will bring the auto accident problem from the lofty reaches of social insurance philosophizing back to the specific problem of auto accidents. Assume for the purposes of analysis that we have a universe in which only auto drivers are ever injured by automobiles.[98] If then we were to compel all motorists to carry liability insurance to cover any damage to others they cause by driving, could it not be said that, whatever we may call this scheme, it functionally and realistically reduces to compulsory accident insurance? Since there is a considerable overlap between drivers and victims of auto accidents, it might appear that on this view the Columbia plan has been transformed into a workable compulsory auto accident insurance scheme for the whole society. One thus might well be tempted to argue that the most persuasive justification for an auto compensation plan may be that it is the only practical way of approximating the goal of compulsory accident insurance without opening up the larger issues inherent in any use of social insurance. And, if so, we appear to reach the perplexity that there is really nothing left to debate as to coverage of victims since all plans, including the common law with compulsory liability insurance, lead to de facto accident insurance schemes.

But the real world is not quite so tidy. The overlap between drivers and victims is far from perfect and it is imperfect enough to leave a substantial number of victims who will be covered by the plan although they

---

[97] But compare James, *supra* note 76, at 415: "And the objection to singling out the automobile approaches the trivial. The automobile accident has singled itself out, as its frequency and economic consequences plainly show. . . . A good case can be made for a much broader type of social insurance, perhaps covering all disabilities from accident or illness. But those who raise the present objection would be the last to espouse anything like that."

[98] See the parallel analysis in Note, *Absolute Liability for Dangerous Things,* 61 HARV. L. REV. 515 (1948).

will not have contributed to the fund. In brief, the motorist who asks why he is being compelled to contribute to the fund for compensating a pedestrian who does not drive in all likelihood will not be reassured by the answer that in effect he is only insuring himself. Moreover, the degree of overlap between drivers and victims in any given time period will not be constant, but will be contingent on various factors such as the age distribution of the population and relative prosperity of the country. And further, there is still a crucial difference between accident insurance and liability insurance when one comes to appraise risks for the purpose of differentiating among insureds in setting premiums. The relevant criterion for rating risks in the case of liability insurance is the propensity of the owner, or those who use his car, to cause accidents; the relevant criterion for rating risks in the case of accident insurance is the propensity of the victim to get hurt. If one believes that the accurate grading of premiums is an important policy consideration in any insurance scheme, then a liability insurance system cannot be made to function like a true accident insurance system.

We cannot resist another comment. If a latent preference for compulsory auto accident insurance is behind the support for compensation plans, it would at least be a great improvement in candor to have this value made explicit.

8

One of the most persistent arguments advanced in behalf of compensation plans is that adoption of a plan would yield sufficient economies to make the coverage for additional victims virtually costless. The contention turns on a very simple thought. The subtlety of the fault criterion and the cumbersomeness of the jury system appear to make the cost of administering the present law very high. It is asserted that the streamlined procedures and rules of compensation plans would make possible a marked reduction in these costs. This savings, it is argued, would be sufficient to pay for the cost of the additional coverage prescribed by the plan.[99]

At the outset it will be helpful to define what is meant by the costs of administering either the present system or any compensation plan. For this purpose, the definition has to be somewhat artificial since we are not dealing with measurements which fit within the familiar analysis of accountants or economists. The most useful definition of these costs has two components: (1) the expenses incurred in transferring compensation dollars to claimants and (2) the compensation dollars paid in satisfaction of

---

[99] See, e.g., Morris, *The Insurance Principle: Compulsory Insurance* in CONFERENCE ON INSURANCE (University of Chicago Law School Conference Series No. 14, 1954).

fraudulent claims. Both components are relevant to the current controversy over plans. Proponents of plans argue that their systems will be less costly than the common law in that plans will transfer a given number of compensation dollars to claimants with the expenditure of a smaller total number of dollars for expenses.[100] Opponents of plans argue that a plan will be more vulnerable to fraudulent claims—admittedly a somewhat subjective concept. The full argument for a compensation plan based on its internal economies is that, as compared to the present system, the savings on transfer costs will greatly outweigh any loss from an increase in fraudulent claims.

We turn to consider the impact of a plan on fraudulent claims.[101] The auto plans do not have anything comparable to the built-in protection surrounding the usual industrial accident covered by workmen's compensation. In the case of the auto accident, witnesses are likely to be more transient, the relationship between the parties is likely to be that of total strangers, and the post-accident evidence is likely to be more elusive. The upshot is that, on the average, it is appreciably more difficult to investigate and determine the legitimacy of the claim in the case of the auto accident than in the case of the industrial accident. The important question here, however, is whether an auto plan will offer a greater inducement to fraudulent claims than the present common law arrangement. Presumably no one is equipped to answer this question with any assurance, but several conjectures might be advanced. It is in the area of the relatively small auto accident claim that fraud today appears to be most prevalent. One might argue that some plans would produce an increase in small claims and by this route an increase in fraud. It might also be argued that because of the change in the basis of liability the opportunities for defeating claims would be substantially lessened under a plan. Insurance carriers[102] consequently might become less active in defending against small claims under a plan, and it is conceivable that a reduced degree of investigation would both encourage the filing of false claims and hinder the detection of frauds. Cutting the other way is the fact that much of the fraud today seems to be associated with the need for establishing the negligence of the driver and the absence of negligence on the part of the victim in order to recover. Under a plan the inducement for such fraud will have been eliminated, in much the fashion that the standard deduction

---

[100] For a comparative analysis of the operating costs of making payments under various benefit systems, including the common law, see Bombaugh, *The Economic Significance of Loss Shifting in the United States*, 28 J. Ins. 13 (1961).

[101] James, *supra* note 76, at 419-20; Lilly, *supra* note 60; Sherman, *Grounds for Opposing the Automobile Accident Compensation Plan*, 3 LAW & CONTEMP. PROB. 598.

[102] Or public officials under the social security model.

in the income tax has lowered the over-all chances for fraud with respect to small itemized deductions.[103]

Our own conclusion from these conjectures is that, although it is possible that the incidence of fraud would increase under a plan, it is unlikely that the fraud loss would bulk large enough to produce a significant change in costs. Accordingly, we shall simplify our discussion of comparative costs by foregoing further concern with the incidence of fraud.

Putting fraud to one side, the crucial question for internal economies is to what extent will a plan reduce the transfer costs that are present in the current system. The relevant comparison is between the total private and official costs of processing all claims for compensation today (whether or not they are in the end paid) and the total private and official costs that would arise under a compensation plan in processing this *same* universe of claims. It is not relevant for present purposes that under a plan additional claims would be filed and compensated because of the expanded coverage. The question is simply whether the plan will succeed in handling more cheaply the claims that are now processed.[104]

It has been contended that a plan would produce such economies because the changes it would make in substantive rules as to liability and damages would significantly reduce the area, intensity and complexity of controversy. The argument is that there would be appreciably less need for official adjudications and for the utilization of experts and their auxiliaries in the settlement process and in the litigation of claims. A savings in official costs would follow in that there would be need for fewer judges, fewer juries, fewer courtrooms and fewer functionaries; and a savings in

103 When the income tax became a mass tax in the early forties, it proved very difficult to police the small claims for deductions which taxpayers were required to itemize. In part to eliminate the "fraud" problem, the law was modified to allow a limited automatic deduction to all taxpayers whether or not they were in a position otherwise to claim specific deductions.

104 A simple numerical example may perhaps be helpful here. Assume that under the common law we have a community which averages 1000 accidents a year and that 600 of these are compensable. Assume further that on the average $500 in damages are paid on each claim and that the processing of claims "costs" $150 per claim.

If under a shift to a plan these costs are reduced from $150 per claim to $50, there will be a savings of $100 $\times$ 600 = $60,000 in the sense that the plan will do what the common law system is doing—namely, processing these 600 accident claims—and will do it more economically.

Further, this economy will be operative even though the shift to a plan will add 400 newly eligible claims.

Under the common law a fund of 600 $\times$ $500 or $300,000 was required to give each of 600 claimants a $500 — $150 = $350 net award. Under a plan, 1000 $\times$ $400 or $400,000 is required to give each of 1000 claimants a $400 — $50 = $350 net award.

The increased cost of the plan, $100,000, reflects both the economy in handling claims and the added cost of additional coverage.

private costs would follow in that lawyers and other professional personnel would be needed on fewer occasions and their work would command lower fees.

We can grant that the ratio of claims settled to claims litigated is likely to increase under a plan, especially if the plan provides a relatively low ceiling on damages. One must, however, be cautious in assessing the consequences of such a change. The settlement ratio is already extremely high—approaching ninety-seven percent for all claims—so that the latitude for savings through this route is rather narrow.[105] There is further the disturbing note that workmen's compensation, which a half century ago offered a comparable promise of holding litigation down to a negligible level, has continued to provide fertile ground for adjudicated controversy. It should also be emphasized that some of the potential savings in official costs are illusory in that we have already paid for the courtrooms, and the judges and functionaries are already on the public payroll and are likely to remain there. And whatever the savings in official costs, there is little likelihood that their magnitude can make much of an impact since the total of such costs attributable to auto accident cases can only be a very small fraction of the total compensation payments made each year as a result of injuries from autos.[106]

The main avenue for achieving a savings in cost is through reduction in the use of the services of experts (and auxiliary personnel) and in the compensation paid for their services. The measure of the savings, as we see it, can perhaps best be explored by centering on the role of lawyers in the compensation process, keeping in mind that investigators, claims agents and other talents are also necessarily involved.

It is often assumed that under a plan the law will become so much clearer and simpler that many more claims will not only stay out of litigation but will be settled by the parties without the intervention of lawyers. We are not that sanguine.[107] There is little basis in experience to justify the prediction. The fact is that in the aggregate we are dealing with transfers of large sums of money, and no matter how much the law is simplified there will always remain an irreducible amount of ambiguity in the rules, as well as doubts as to the facts in particular cases. As long as any disagreements remain, with a dollar value attached to their resolution, we can expect that the process of disposing of claims will not be

---

105 ZEISEL, KALVEN & BUCHHOLZ, DELAY IN THE COURT, pt. III (1959).

106 A boundary figure is provided in the careful estimate that $200,000,000 a year changes hands as a result of personal injury accidents in New York City. Franklin, Chanin & Mark, *Accidents, Money and the Law: A Study of the Economics of Personal Injury Litigation*, 61 COLUM. L. REV. 1, 14 (1961).

107 For a vigorous defense of the role of the lawyer in processing workmen's compensation claims, see Marcus, *Advocating the Rights of the Injured*, 61 MICH. L. REV. 921 (1963).

automatic or effortless. In operating a plan, moreover, a high degree of expertise is bound to develop on the side of the fund, the administration of which inevitably will take on all the characteristics of a large bureaucracy. Most claimants are likely to perceive the need for equally qualified experts to represent them in negotiations. Thus on both sides there will be a demand for expert services which cannot be wholly eliminated. There will be situations, to be sure, under a plan where individual claimants will attempt to perform this service function on their own behalf where they would not do so today. Even in these instances, however, there is a danger of overstating the reduction in costs. While it is true that a claimant would then not have to pay for the services of an expert, it is equally true that he incurs the cost of his own services. The perception of this as a cost is not just a nicety of the economist; the claimant is investing his own time, and in many cases it would be more economical for him to pay for an expert and to use his own time otherwise. All things considered, it is extremely improbable that the compensation system can be simplified to such an extent that virtually no time or effort would be involved in obtaining payment of claims.

Further, we should not rush to applaud the apparent enthusiasm here for killing off the lawyers. We suggest that in a substantial number of cases, even where the value of the claimant's time is a matter of indifference, he will be financially better off with good legal representation. Everything in our experience strongly indicates that the lawyer frequently is an economically valuable component of the negotiating process in the simple sense that the results are different when he participates. For a compensation plan to work as intended, the adversary balance contributed by the lawyer will often be needed.

In spite of our reservations, it must be admitted that no one can predict with confidence what the new patterns of behavior in processing claims would be like under a plan. New customs, departing from strictly economic behavior, might easily develop. Our semi-educated guess is that the services of lawyers would continue in fairly heavy demand. Experience with workmen's compensation, although not precisely analogous, heavily underscores this conclusion.

It may also be contended by the proponents of plans that a major part of the reduction in lawyer costs would be in the form of a price reduction. Lawyers, in brief, would charge less under a plan than under present conditions. Because settlements are so large a fraction of dispositions today, and presumably would be even larger under a plan, the main point for inquiry is not whether lawyers would charge less for trying cases than they do today but whether they would charge less for presenting and settling claims than they do today.

In tracing out whether lawyers would charge less, some elementary economic notions are relevant. If they charge less under a plan, it must either be due to voluntary choice or because fees are regulated. Absent government regulations, the explanation of lower fees under a plan must be either that lawyers feel a moral obligation to charge less or that market forces are altered. Both explanations must ultimately rest on the point that the challenge confronting the lawyer in auto claims has been greatly simplified by the plan.[108] It does not appear to us fruitful to explore the morality of the voluntary fee setting process; we see no reason why the lawyer in our society should not be governed by the dictates of the market in setting fees, and in passing we cannot resist observing that adherence to market criteria would result in the most economic allocation of legal talent among alternative uses. Thus the issue is reduced to whether the changes made by a plan would alter market conditions for the supply and demand of legal services in connection with compensation claims. We have already concluded that while the demand for such services might be diminished, the reduction is not likely to be major. If the price of legal services is to be drastically changed through market forces, it must be because of alterations on the supply side. The argument that change will occur is that the operation of a plan would call for less skill on the part of lawyers in handling claims and therefore more lawyers would possess the degree of skill needed to compete for this type of business. This line of analysis is plausible as far as it goes, but we must remember that we understand little about the economic structure of the personal injury bar today. It is hard to see that scarcity of roughly comparable talent alone accounts for the notably high remuneration received by the top tort lawyers.

More likely, what the proponents of plans have had in mind regarding lower fees is much simpler—the plan would by government decree fix fee levels. No doubt such regulation could have the effect of reducing fees in compensation cases, although in the long run it might also have repercussions on how legal talent was allocated between compensation claims and demands for legal services that are unregulated. But what is of immediate interest is this question: What is there about a plan which justifies making a particular change we apparently would not make absent a plan? Specifically, in what way does a plan justify fixing fees? Insofar as the impetus for regulation comes from a feeling that lawyers now charge too much, all that can be said is that the plan is being used as an occasion to precipitate a change which otherwise would be difficult to bring about. Nor is it sound to urge that under a plan fees should be

108 And, of course, the contingency of liability has been eliminated.

regulated because the lawyer would no longer be performing as valuable a service. While this contention might form a basis for criticising the bar if it charged the same fees under a plan as before, it cannot explain why we are unwilling to rely on the market to set fee levels under a plan whereas we are willing in general to trust the market under present conditions.

In any event, some perspective on the magnitudes involved here is needed. We have already noted that the potential savings in official costs is relatively trivial. Lawyers' fees for claimants appear to run about a third of the total settlements.[109] Making the most favorable assumption that fees would be controlled and limited to half that fraction, such regulation could produce a reduction in charges equal roughly to fifteen percent of total payments on claims. The potential for financing additional coverage via this route can be no greater.

It is important to make explicit here the steps by which these savings in private costs, unlike any savings in official costs, are thought to become available to finance additional coverage. In simplest form the contention is as follows: Of the gross awards today under the common law, about two-thirds is taken home by claimants and the balance goes to pay for fees and other private costs. It is assumed that by simplifying the whole process, a compensation plan will bring about a 50% reduction in fees and other private costs. If the award level under a plan is lowered by the equivalent of this 50% reduction, claimants on the average would receive the same take-home awards as before, and hence as a class would not suffer as a result of the shift to a plan. If the money that previously went into the higher lawyers' fees and other private costs were used to provide coverage for additional victims, motorists would not be called upon to pay in the aggregate any more than under the common law, and hence also would not be any worse off under the plan. In brief, this approach to a plan provides additional coverage for victims at no extra cost to anyone, except possibly the lawyers.

It remains to examine the assumption that the savings in private costs should be devoted to financing coverage for additional victims. We previously questioned the logic of giving the benefits of lower awards to a new class of victims instead of to motorists. Similarly, should not the savings in private costs be used to reduce the costs borne by motorists or, if not, should not the savings at least be used to increase the take-home awards of the victims who recover at common law? On first impression, the use of the savings to finance additional coverage seems like an un-

109 Franklin, Chanin & Mark, *supra* note 106, at 21. For all cases in New York City in 1957, the average fee was 36%.

justifiable step. To borrow from an illustration we introduced earlier,[110] let us assume that road maintenance has been financed by a special tax on gasoline. An innovation in technology cuts in half the cost of maintenance. The question is whether these savings should be available for other public purposes, such as the maintenance of schools, or whether in justice the benefits should accrue to those who pay the special gasoline tax. To restate our prior conclusion, it seems pretty clear that tax reduction is the appropriate solution. Does this analogy hold for the savings in costs expected from internal economies in changing to a compensation plan?

The answer is somewhat striking. There seems to be no way of giving these savings to motorists in lieu of having a plan, because on hypothesis the savings in costs cannot be had in the absence of a plan. There is a comparable difficulty in passing the savings on to the victims who would have recovered at common law, so as to increase their take-home awards. These savings, again on hypothesis, are realized only if there is a plan, and in this context the assumption is that there will be a plan only because these savings are available to finance it.

Thus the internal economies approach furnishes a strong argument for extending the coverage as required by a compensation plan, provided only that the magnitude of the savings is great enough to finance the additional coverage and that there is no new offsetting factor which might erase the savings.

Whatever the range of plausible estimates might be, there will be one offsetting factor which casts a long shadow over the hope that there will be sufficient net savings to finance the additional coverage. A favorite argument of insurance industry spokesmen is that a plan will result in a radical increase in claims consciousness. It is necessary to trace through this challenge with some care.

As a first step we should distinguish between an increase in claims consciousness and an increase in fraud. We have already dealt with the impact of plans on fraud. Our concern here is with any increase in the propensity to file non-fraudulent claims. It is also important not to confuse the point under consideration with the increase in coverage, and hence the addition of claims by newly covered victims, that will be a chief feature of any plan. Speaking precisely, an increase in claims consciousness refers to a shift in the attitude of accident victims with respect to their willingness to bear marginal or trivial or doubtful (but not fraudulent) losses themselves, rather than attempt to shift such losses by filing claims. One might expect that there would be

110 See section 3 *supra* at pages 23-24.

a stable propensity to file claims whenever possible. However, there is striking evidence that the ratio of claims filed for personal injuries varies markedly over different parts of the country.[111] These findings suggest strongly that the filing of claims is influenced by subtle cultural or psychological forces, and therefore that a large-scale change in institutions and legal rules might well alter the existing claims ratio.

A variety of factors may affect the claims ratio: (1) the ease of pursuing a claim; (2) the estimate of the actual likelihood of official scrutiny; (3) the degree of organized exploiting or stimulating of claims; and (4) the community mores with respect to the propriety of victims absorbing marginal losses themselves. Avowedly we have no empirical studies on how a plan would affect these four factors, but it would appear that under most plans all four are likely to change in a direction which increases the filing of claims. The costs of pursuing a claim must have some direct relationship to whether it is filed, and these costs, which include not only the fees for services of expert intermediaries but also the personal costs of engaging in controversy, will presumably go down. The difficulties of official scrutiny will increase as the volume of claims, particularly small ones, increases and this difficulty is likely to be perceived widely by the community, thus acting as an invitation to file claims. As the settlement of claims becomes easier, more persons may be tempted to engage in soliciting them, with the likelihood that fewer marginal claims will escape notice. And finally, and perhaps most important, the whole tone of the society with respect to the decencies of shifting losses off oneself is likely to change. If the plan has been promoted in terms of compensating all who are injured—that is, as awarding something to which a man is entitled simply because he is a victim—we may expect a diminution in reticence to pursue a small or an ambiguous claim.

We would conclude that it is most probable that the introduction of a plan would bring with it a marked increase in claims consciousness. What follows from this?

We should first note that the expansibility of the claims universe is only a short-run phenomenon. During the transitional years, it is likely to be extremely difficult to predict the total level of claims on the basis of any prior experience. Understandably this would complicate the problems of the insurance industry in pricing and marketing coverage. At the end of the transition period, however, a new equilibrium would be reached because the factors which initially stimulated an increase in claims consciousness would presumably remain constant once the plan had been adopted. The new degree of claims consciousness would provide

---

[111] Zeisel, Kalven & Buchholz, Delay in the Court, ch. 20 (1959).

a reasonably secure base to the insurance industry for projecting the higher future level of claims.

It is precisely because this new equilibrium is likely to be at a higher level that there well may be an offset to the savings from internal economies of a plan. As we have seen, a compensation plan might be able to make more funds available for payment of claims by handling any given number of claims more economically than the common law would handle them. The savings can only be had by adopting a plan. But we now see that the very adoption of a plan would not only add new claimants because of the expanded coverage, but would enlarge the number of claims filed because of an increase in claims consciousness. It is obvious that the monies needed to satisfy the claims arising from an increase in claims consciousness would pro tanto not be available to finance the new coverage sought by the plan. Thus the very change to a plan which produces economies in handling claims is likely to produce a stimulus for proliferating claims. While no estimates of the magnitudes are available,[112] it is conceivable that a compensation plan would have to run faster to stay in the same place.[113]

The difficulty, then, with this approach to a compensation plan is that it asks us to balance one conjecture against another.

There is a concluding observation which is common to both the internal economies approach to financing a plan and the approach via reallocating damages among victims. Both have, as a characteristic feature, the promise that the additional coverage will be financed without imposing additional costs on motorists. We can look upon this as a kind of bargain with motorists under which they would trade their liability at common law for their strict but limited liability under the plan. If this rhetoric of a bargain is to be treated as an important part of the rationale for a plan, it becomes relevant to ask whether the bargain can be kept.

The bargain envisages collecting a fund on the basis of going insurance rates and using the size of the fund as a yardstick to fix the magnitude of benefits. One need not be a total skeptic to conclude that such a bargain might be difficult to maintain. In practice, it likely will turn out that over time, the magnitude of the benefits will be redetermined and that costs then will be reassessed so as to finance the new level of payouts.

---

112 In New York City the maximum increase in claims would be 13%, given the estimate that only 13% of accidents are not followed by claims. HUNTING & NEUWIRTH, WHO SUES IN NEW YORK CITY (1962). New York City, however, is a very claims conscious area. ZEISEL, KALVIN & BUCHHOLZ, DELAY IN THE COURT, ch. 20 (1959).

113 Claims awareness, it can well be argued, is not necessarily bad. On this view, the point would simply be that the costs of "properly" compensating for auto accidents are larger than we would anticipate on the basis of experience under the common law system.

After a few years it will become impossible to reconstruct the baseline, and thus all traces of the original terms of the bargain will have been lost. In the end a large part of the increased burden is likely to be put on motorists, with the change occurring under circumstances that foreclose discussion of the policy which is involved.

9

We now reach a fourth and last stage in our analysis of alternative ways of handling the cost of additional coverage in compensation plans. The three alternatives examined so far have had in common that no new costs would be charged to owners or operators of vehicles; rather, additional coverage was to be financed either by having the victims insure themselves, or by redistributing awards among victims, or by effectuating internal economies in administering claims. Yet the most common way of thinking about plans has been to assume that increased coverage is at least in part to be financed by motorists.[114] Often the policy issue that would be posed by adding costs onto motorists is passed over by arguing that this issue is premature until we know how much the plan will cost after it has actually been in operation. We believe that the issue can be posed sharply without knowing how much the plan will cost. The policy question is: If the expanded coverage in operation will cost more than the present system, what justification is there for placing such additional costs on those who own or operate vehicles?

It is worth recalling the obvious here concerning the common law. The ready answer of the common law is that whatever costs are attributable to the negligence of motorists should be placed on them absent contributory negligence on the part of victims. This answer is, by definition, not available in the case of plans, which reject fault as the exclusive criterion for shifting accident losses. The critical question thus can be restated: What criterion other than fault can justify putting the cost of additional coverage on motorists?

In recent years the fashionable response has been that one should look to economic analysis.[115] We here reach an appropriate place to ask: What can economic theory contribute to the development of liability theory? The formula which the academic commentator appears to have borrowed from the economist is that the loss should be placed on the superior risk

---

114 See, for example, the Columbia Plan, *supra* note 6; the Ehrenzweig Plan, *supra* note 9; and the Green Plan, *supra* note 13.

115 EHRENZWEIG, NEGLIGENCE WITHOUT FAULT (1951); Calabresi, *Some Thoughts on Risk Distribution and the Law of Torts*, 70 YALE L.J. 499 (1961); James, *Accident Liability Reconsidered: The Impact of Liability Insurance*, 57 YALE L.J. 549 (1948); Keeton, *Conditional Fault in the Law of Torts*, 72 HARV. L. REV. 401 (1959); Morris, *Hazardous Enterprises and Risk Bearing Capacity*, 61 YALE L.J. 1172 (1952).

bearer. It has frequently been noted that this is a phrase which is rich in ambiguity, and we suspect it might well be disowned by the economist. But for present purposes at least three meanings—two minor and one major—can be isolated and examined in the context of compensation plans.

The bluntest version, which echoes early discussion of vicarious liability doctrines, is that the loss should be placed on the party with the "deepest pocket."[116] Whatever the merits of the deep pocket view generally, there are some special difficulties with it as applied to auto accidents. Motorists, the argument runs, should pay for accident losses because as a class they are wealthier than victims as a class. In our society most automobiles belong to individuals and not to business organizations. While early in the auto era, and especially in the horse and buggy days, the average vehicle owner was surely wealthier than the average victim, there is reason to doubt that this proposition is meaningfully true today. Certainly it must be true that many victims are wealthier than many motorists, and certainly there must be wide variations in wealth both among motorists and among victims. We are therefore reduced to dealing with averages of some kind. Even if such averages were available to us, there would be the question of how big a difference in the averages is significant for deep pocket purposes. And the argument is further embarrassed by the considerable overlap between those who drive cars and those who are auto accident victims.[117]

But let us assume for the sake of argument that there is a significant difference between the two groups—that only drivers of solid gold Cadillacs ever injure people and that only those in the bottom fourth of the income scale are ever victims. Would the deep pocket argument then be persuasive? The appeal of the principle is that it redistributes wealth or income so as to reduce economic inequalities. As a method of redistribution, however, it confronts several difficulties. Redistribution from motorists to victims necessarily will act like a regressive tax among motorists. Not all owners of solid gold Cadillacs will have identical amounts of income or wealth, and if each is required to pay the same premium for compensation insurance every year, there will be not only a redistribution from the very rich to the very poor but also a redistribution from the less wealthy to the more wealthy. A solid gold Cadillac, in brief, is an

116 Baty, Vicarious Liability 154 (1916); Ehrenzweig, *Assurance Oblige—A Comparative Study*, 15 Law & Contemp. Prob. 445 (1950).

The famous Baty phrase is followed by these two sentences: "The present is not a very propitious time for withstanding a dogma based on such a principle. But a return to simpler manners will probably bring with it a return to saner views of liability, even if it is not sooner recognized that to injure capital is to injure industry."

117 See section 7 *supra*.

unnecessarily imprecise index of wealth or income. The whole venture would be somewhat reminiscent of the old English tax predicated on the number of windows in one's dwelling.

We need not belabor the point. While a progressive general tax on income, wealth or expenditure can redistribute income or wealth among individuals or families in a meaningful, if uneasy, manner, car ownership or ownership of other specific assets is not likely to be a satisfactory substitute. A general tax system can implement systematic decisions about the inequalities of income or wealth in society. If, however, every price in the society were set with an eye to the wealth or income of users, the result could only be chaotic. The fallacy of the deep pocket approach in this context is an old one: It is not feasible for the law adequately to solve problems of distributive justice when dealing with problems of corrective justice.

The second meaning of the superior risk bearer formula is less crude but hardly more helpful. The idea is that whoever has superior access to insurance is the superior risk bearer.[118] This concept of superior risk-bearing was developed primarily to throw light on judge-made common law rules. In that context it sometimes made sense for the court to look to the insurance habits and customs of the community and then to devise a rule of liability that best reflected them. However, when we move to the level of legislative decision, these guide lines lose their significance. The relevant question becomes: Who should be compelled to carry the insurance? While a court, in justifying its liability rule, cannot dictate new patterns of insuring but can consider only existing habits, the legislature has great latitude in dictating what "customs" it wants to establish as to the carrying of insurance.[119]

It is an undoubted fact that the custom of carrying liability insurance is much wider among motorists than is the custom of carrying accident insurance among victims. What support does this offer, at the level of legislative discretion, for putting additional costs on motorists? It is shortsighted to look only at current insurance habits. We must recall again that it is the public at large that constitutes the universe of potential victims and there is nothing that prevents the legislature from in effect compelling nearly everyone to carry accident insurance through extension of the social security system. The real question then becomes: With respect to access to insurance, are motorists as a class superior risk bearers

[118] Ehrenzweig, *Assurance Oblige—A Comparative Study*, 15 LAW & CONTEMP. PROB. 445 (1950); Morris, *Hazardous Enterprises and Risk Bearing Capacity*, 61 YALE L.J. 1172 (1952).

[119] See generally GREGORY & KALVEN, CASES ON TORTS, ch. 10 (1959), and especially 634-41.

to the tax paying public? The very existence of social security indicates that the answer is obviously no.

The third—and surely the most important—meaning of the superior risk bearer formula is that enterprises should pay their own way. Beginning with the celebrated analyses of vicarious liability a generation ago, a whole series of legal problems have been re-analyzed from this perspective.[120] Under this approach those interested in law in effect turn to the economist for advice in the expectation that the economist's analyses regarding the allocation of costs will aid the law in reaching determinations on the allocation of liability. As far as we can tell, many in the legal world have thought that the concept of an enterprise paying its own way offers a sufficient bridge into the world of economics.[121] They hear the economist talking about proper and improper allocation of costs and understand him as saying that an improper allocation of costs leads to an uneconomic and impolitic result. The lawyer's expectation is that by translating the liability issue into a question of costs, he can draw on the expertise of the economist to reach a proper allocation of these costs.

But if the economist is patient and candid, the lawyer will find his great expectations shaken. The economist will point out that the allocation of costs is not a matter of giving a description of the facts of the economic order, as the lawman seems to have thought. Rather the allocation of costs is always avowedly instrumental. Only if we specify the goals can the economist tell us what is the proper allocation of costs.

But the possibility of getting help from the economist does not end so abruptly. The lawyer may well find congenial two goals which are commonly found in the writings of economists: (1) It is desirable to arrange matters so that as many decisions as possible about the use of resources are made responsive to realistic voting by the consumers of goods and services; (2) in satisfying the votes of consumers, given the existing distribution of wealth and income, it is desirable to maximize output through achieving the most efficient combinations of resources. Using these goals, the economist is now able to say something significant about allocating costs. It is desirable to have consumers confront as realistically as possible the costs of activities in choosing among alternatives. And it is preferable to place costs strategically on those whose decisions can affect the magnitude of the costs. The first injunction will tend to make

---

[120] See, e.g., Douglas, *Vicarious Liability and Administration of Risk*, 38 YALE L.J. 584, 720 (1929); Laski, *The Basis of Vicarious Liability*, 26 YALE L.J. 105 (1916); Seavey, *Speculations as to "Respondeat Superior,"* in HARVARD LEGAL ESSAYS 433 (1934); Smith, *Frolic and Detour*, 23 COLUM. L. REV. 444, 716 (1923); Steffen, *Independent Contractor and the Good Life*, 2 U. CHI. L. REV. 501 (1935).

[121] *Cf.* Smith, *supra* note 120.

the allocation of resources in the society conform to the free choice of the members expressed through the market. The second injunction will tend to hold down waste and maximize efficiency in producing the goods and services for which the consumers have voted.[122]

Assuming that we accept these twin goals as stating an attractive public policy, what advice can the economist now give us about resolving liability issues? To convey an adequate sense of the framework for economic analysis, it will be convenient to pause and consider liability problems somewhat more generously and not limit ourselves to the auto accident situation. Avowedly we will be exploring the matter in greater detail than is required by our specific topic. The justification, if one is needed, is that the idiom of economic analysis has been widely imported into legal literature in what now strikes us as being an incomplete and confusing way.

The world of liability is concerned with injury to persons and property.[123] There should be little difficulty in seeing that such injuries destroy or impair scarce resources and are therefore costs. Looking at these costs through the economist's eyes, a key distinction for the law and for theories of enterprise liability emerges. The distinction might be best approached by a simple example. Let us suppose that a certain radioactive material on the face of a wristwatch dial causes skin damage to some persons who wear the watch. The important characteristics of this situation are that users of the watch acquired the product in voluntary market transactions with the manufacturer and that only users of the watch are exposed to the harm. Thus the universe of consumer voters and the universe of potential victims coincide.

In this situation the economist can add a major insight to what the lawyer might normally perceive about the relationships involved. If the law imposes liability for the harm from the watch dials on the manufacturer, that cost ultimately will be reflected in the price of the watches and hence the cost will be borne by the consumers of the product. Legal writing in recent years has picked up this point and often takes the position that, whenever possible, liability costs should be placed on an indus-

---

122 We are asserting that in our use of economic analysis in this section, nothing turns on whether an industry is highly competitive or monopolistic. See Calabresi, *supra* note 115.

It should be emphasized that we are concerned only with long-run analysis. We are ignoring the economic consequences which might occur in the short-run if the society were to move from one liability rule to another.

123 For reasons of simplicity we have omitted explicit discussion of damages to property. While the Columbia Plan did not cover property claims, we are assuming that the various models of plans under discussion could be extended to cover injury to property without changing any essential features of the analysis.

try in order to achieve such wide distribution of loss. This, however, is only half the story as the economist tells it. If the law does not impose liability on the manufacturer of the watches but leaves it on the consumers, the result would again be that consumers as a class bear the loss. The risk of harm from using the watch, it may be assumed, will be known to users and they will regard it as part of the cost of the product. Therefore whether liability is placed on the industry or the loss is left with consumers, the economy will be equally responsive to consumer voting and consumers as a class will cast the same vote. The law's choice of liability rules thus would seem to have no impact on the allocation of resources in the society. To the economist, the choice of legal rule for this situation might seem prima facie to be a matter of indifference.

On further analysis this is not quite the case. But the difference in consequences is not what the lawyer might have expected. Placing liability on the industry is tantamount to compelling the consumers to buy insurance against the loss through paying a higher price. The outcome would be that each user would purchase not only the product but also insurance against harm from the product, in much the same way that today he frequently is forced to purchase "free" trading stamps. This obviously is a sure method for bringing about total insurance coverage against the harm for all purchasers of the product. For a variety of reasons it can be argued that the coverage would not be the same if the law were to leave the loss with consumers. As a practical matter, accident insurance may not be available for so narrowly defined a risk; the consumers may perceive the risk of harm differently than does the industry; and many consumers may deliberately elect not to insure themselves. But such differences in insurance coverage need not lead us to the conclusion that it is better policy for the law to place the cost on the industry. For one thing, this automatic form of compulsory insurance in effect provides every consumer with the same coverage at the same price. It therefore cannot adjust adequately to the differing insurance needs of individual consumers of the product, with the result that some will overpay and others will underpay for protection.[124] And, more important, like any form of compulsory insurance, it deprives the consumer of his own choice as to whether he wishes to carry insurance.[125]

While considerably more could be said about the competing considerations in this situation, what is arresting for us is that the whole issue turns on the merits of compulsory accident insurance. The statement of

[124] In theory at least, numerous personal factors might affect sharply the rational need for such accident insurance. Age is a good example.

[125] The fact that the consumer cannot buy the product without buying "the insurance" may itself have an impact on the allocation of resources in the society.

the policy issue now has an unfamiliar ring.[126] In the end the argument for strict liability turns out to be that it provides the most strategic method for compelling accident insurance.

Having stayed with the economist this far, and perhaps having been reassured by learning that so little depends on the choice of liability rules, we come back to the problem of auto accidents. Does the same analysis hold? If it is thought to be a good idea to place the cost of radium dial injuries on the industry to spread losses, is it not an equally good idea to place the cost of auto accidents on car manufacturers or motorists?

The economist will tell us that here the choice of liability rule may entail consequences of a different order. In his scheme of things, the injuries caused by autos and the radium dial injuries involve intrinsically different situations. Unlike our watch illustration, the risk of harm from autos is not confined to those who buy and drive cars, but includes also those who are strangers to the marketing and use of autos. Insofar as this is true, the cost of auto accidents will not inescapably be borne by motorists through the voluntary act of purchasing or driving a car. The upshot is that under the economist's value system it will make a difference where the law places the loss. If placed on motorists, the loss becomes a cost of driving. If left on victims, the loss is what the economist might call an "externality" to the auto industry—a cost to society but not one to producers or users of cars.[127] The size of the auto industry, and hence the allocation of resources, can be expected to be materially different under the two alternative legal rules.

At this point it would appear that the economist does find the legal question significant, and that here, unlike the radium watch dial case,

<hr>

[126] Compare, however, the discussion in section 7 *supra,* pages 40 *et seq.*

[127] A more precise statement of the distinctions that the economist draws among costs is as follows:

1. Arbitrary costs—those not resulting from the voluntary exchange of resources and voluntary use of products. Instances are taxes and subsidies.
2. Non-arbitrary costs—those resulting from the voluntary exchange of resources and voluntary use of products.
   (A) Internal costs—payments required to get the voluntary cooperation of productive factors and costs imposed on the buyer by the voluntary act of use. These costs necessarily rest with the user in a voluntary exchange economy.
   (B) Externality costs—costs arising from the interaction of social units with the production or use process where these social units are not involved in voluntary cooperation with the producer or user.

The clear distinction in theory between the two kinds of non-arbitrary costs may sometimes blur in reality. On certain assumptions even the costs in the radium watch dial instance can be viewed as "externalities." Thus suppose the loss is left on the consumers rather than the industry, and it is borne at least in part not by them but by some form of welfare plan to which they do not contribute at all.

the law can make a mistake in economics. But once again the promise of a decisive contribution from economics to legal policy slips from our grasp. In order to know when the law distorts consumer voting in the allocation of resources, we must first know which group of consumers should properly confront the cost of auto accidents. If auto accidents are properly a cost of using autos but the law elects to leave auto accident losses on the victims, there will be a resulting distortion in the allocation of resources. If auto accidents are not properly a cost of using autos but a cost of some other activity—perhaps of living in general—and if the law elects to shift auto accident losses to the users of autos, there will be a comparable distortion in the allocation of resources. In this perplexing situation can the economist advise us where the costs of auto accidents properly belong? The answer seems to be no. Nothing in his analysis can inform us whether it is less arbitrary to place the auto accident losses on the drivers or to leave them with the victims. Economics, in short, cannot tell us under which legal rule we run the larger risk of distortion.[128]

The root difficulty here is simple and can easily be illustrated by juxtaposing pedestrians and motorists. Whatever can be said about accidents being a consequence of the activity of driving can be said with equal force about accidents being a consequence of the activity of pedestrianism.[129] It is true that we can make a statistical statement that for every so many autos on the road there will be so many auto accidents. But the embarrassment is that one can just as correctly make a statistical statement that for a certain amount of pedestrian activity there will be so many auto accidents. Auto accidents appear to be impregnably a cost of multiple activities.

We seem then, and all too quickly, to have reached an impasse where we cannot use the economist's criteria to resolve our liability issue. But again the economist's stance is not quite so negative. He may offer at least two further observations on which legal rule is preferable.

Recent economic theorizing, associated with the name of Ronald Coase, might alter the picture.[130] It had long been assumed that in the

---

[128] It should be noted that we have analyzed the matter thus far only from the standpoint of the first of the economist's two criteria. We discuss the second at pages 62-64 *infra*.

[129] Or of road building, tire manufacturing, shoe repairing, etc. See Morris, *Enterprise Liability and the Actuarial Process*, 70 YALE L.J. 554 (1961).

But James would dissent; see *The Columbia Study of Compensation for Automobile Accidents: An Unanswered Challenge*, 59 COLUM. L. REV. 408, 415 (1959): "Of course, automobile owners are not engaged in a joint venture for profit, but they do represent the class of people who benefit directly from motoring and who—like the ultimate consumers of the employer's products—may fairly be asked to contribute to the losses which their common activity of motoring causes."

[130] Coase, *The Problem of Social Cost*, 3 J. LAW & ECON. 1 (1960).

situations where the law had a choice of placing a cost on an activity or of leaving it as an externality to that activity, the decision would inevitably affect the allocation of resources. Coase has argued that if the actors and victims—that is, the relevant parties—are free to negotiate with each other and there are no inhibiting costs in bargaining, the result of their negotiation will be the same allocation of resources regardless of where the law places the cost. Insofar as this analysis holds, it suggests that once again, as in the watch dial example, the law cannot make a serious mistake in an economic sense in its choice of liability rule. But unfortunately this reassurance is not likely to be forthcoming for solution of the auto accident problem. It is extremely awkward to imagine motorists and potential victims negotiating about their patterns of activity, and it would seem near fantasy to imagine what the terms of any bargain between them might be. As to the allocation of resources, in the case of auto accidents the law can still make mistakes in selecting a liability rule.

The second qualification turns on a long established point of economic analysis which admittedly we have thus far underplayed. We have been testing alternative legal rules primarily in terms of responsiveness to consumer voting. It is time to deal more directly with the other major goal of economists which at the outset we accepted—maximizing efficiency in satisfying wants by reducing unnecessary costs or waste. For this purpose the important consideration is bringing about the largest net reduction in costs for the entire economy while it responds to consumer demand. In the auto accident situation the question becomes whether the choice of liability rule will make a difference in total costs. This depends not only on whether, as a result of a given rule, there will be a reduction in accidents, but also on how expensive the means used to accomplish this reduction will be. In these terms the argument for putting the loss from accidents on motorists is that it will hold to a minimum the total net costs of accidents to society.

This thesis, although stated in economic idiom, reintroduces us to an old legal friend—deterrence. Generally speaking the law has not taken very seriously the possibility of deterring with tort sanctions. While imposing liability on drivers might cause some people to decide not to drive at all, the law has not been sanguine about the impact of liability on the specific driving behavior of those who do drive.[131] Even apart from the complications introduced by liability insurance,[132] legal commentary has long emphasized that the driver's own personal safety is almost certain to be involved in any accident and that financial liability

---

131 GREGORY & KALVEN, CASES ON TORTS 690-702 (1959); Netherton, *Highway Safety Under Differing Types of Liability Legislation*, 15 OHIO ST. L.J. 110 (1954).
132 See *infra* pages 69-70.

on the driver is not likely to add materially to this natural sanction. It is quite possible that legal commentary has come to this conclusion too quickly and that there are many situations in the auto world in which imposition of liability adds a significant stimulus to prudence on the part of motorists. But there is no need for us to pursue further the troubled issue of deterrence; it is more profitable to turn to other aspects of the economist's quest for a liability rule that will hold down waste.

A major difficulty here is that the thesis requires predictions about behavior of two populations and not just one. It is not enough to predict that if liability is placed on drivers they will act somewhat differently and that there will be a net reduction in costs. This prediction must be weighed against a companion prediction about the reduction in costs if losses are not shifted to drivers but are left on victims. Conceivably investigation might some day establish that there would be a significant difference in the cost reducing potential of those two alternatives for handling accident losses. But surely today no one claims to know this much about the behavior sequences which would be involved. If we are to resort to armchair guessing, the considerations on the one side seem closely balanced by those on the other.

In seeking to use the waste reducing criterion, we have been posing the liability issue in the broad terms of whether all auto accident losses should be placed on drivers or whether all losses should be left on victims. The precise issue is much narrower. Many losses today are shifted by the common law to drivers; what we are seeking to find in economics is whether there is justification for shifting the remaining losses onto drivers. Until now we have considered deterrence without distinguishing between the possible impact of liability rules on faulty conduct and on conduct without fault. Whatever little we may know about deterrence, it seems plausible that liability rules will have a more marked impact on accidents due to fault than on those not caused by fault.[133] If this is accepted, the common law appears to have reached a solution which the economist might find very bright indeed. Offhand, the common law, with its negligence and contributory negligence rules, seems to be maximizing the waste reducing potential of liability rules. it presents inducements to both drivers and potential victims to be careful.

As a final observation on the quest for a liability rule which will most economically reduce waste, it may be asked whether this is, in the end, a prudent way of looking at liability problems. In its efforts to reduce harmful behavior the law, of course, is not limited to tort sanctions. In the auto field we can and do use criminal penalties and licensing con-

---

[133] Compare RESTATEMENT, TORTS § 520, comment g (1934).

trols on drivers. Their availability affects the analysis. If, for example, the case for strict liability on drivers on waste grounds rests in part on the prediction that it will tend to keep poor drivers off the roads, the argument becomes much less persuasive when the availability of these other sanctions is taken into account. Compared with the alternative sanctions, tort liability conceivably might turn out to be the most expensive, as well as the least precise, way of holding down waste due to accidents.[134]

This extended excursion into economic analysis has accepted the twin criteria of having consumers confront proper cost alternatives in casting their votes, and maximizing output of goods and services in response to those votes. It is worth emphasizing that the difficulties we have been experiencing in finding economic clues for legal policy have all arisen in applying these criteria to the problem of allocating liability for harms. We now turn to ask whether these two economic criteria standing alone can *ever* provide a sufficient definition of public policy for the law.

The economist would be the first to warn us that his criteria may not be sufficient for the law. In addition to the goals he has considered, there is a basic question of equity that the law cannot escape the obligation to answer. In simplest form it is, who should be made poorer as a result of

---

[134] The tort sanction coupled with compulsory insurance tends to price driving out of the market for some. This total cessation of driving can be regarded as a cost or expense of this route to accident prevention when compared to methods which would simply reduce careless driving or reduce driving without eliminating it.

After our text was in final form, we received a copy of an unpublished paper by Simon Rottenburg entitled Liability in Law and Economics, dealing with the question "What is the optimal rule for the compensation of persons damaged by accident?" His statement of the economist's goal in accident prevention is illuminating: "Putting to one side ethical questions implicit in the compensation principle, the primary economic object of a liability rule applied to activities causing personal injuries or death is the prevention of accidents, and this because either of these occurrences deprives society of the output the injured or dead person may have produced had the accident not occurred.

"The social purpose is served by the contrivance of incentives for the prevention of accidents or for the prevention of injuries when accidents do occur. The incidence of accidents is a partial negative function of the quantity of resources devoted to accident-prevention. The larger the incentive, the larger will be the quantity of resources put to this use and the smaller will be the number of accidents. The incentive may take the form of costs imposed upon those whose behavior causes accidents. But it is unlikely that the social welfare is maximized by the prevention of *all* accidents because the cost of achieving a zero incidence would undoubtedly be too great. What is wanted is the use, in preventing accidents, of that quantity of resources such that the value of the extra resources used to save the marginal life is equal to the value of that life and the equi-marginal condition is satisfied. Then a unit of resources put to this use will have the same yield as in any other. Yield is measured, in this case, by the expected output of the marginal life saved, net of the expected lifetime consumption of the relevant person, discounted at an appropriate time rate. If either less or more resources are put to this use than is implied by this principle, there is social waste. Either too few or too many accidents occur, too few or too many injuries or deaths ensue, and, given the cost, too much or too little of otherwise lost output is retained."

an accident loss? On this issue the economist once again will find helpful the distinction between inescapable user costs involved in the radium watch dial situation and auto accident injuries which can be externalities to purchasing or using a car. In the former case the economist can reassure us that, as between consumers of watches as a class and the watch industry, the choice of legal rules as to liability does not pose an equity problem since the cost cannot be taken off the users. In the latter case the economist will confirm what the law has long recognized—that its choice of liability rule will make either victims as a class or motorists as a class poorer. This issue of justice is one on which our hypothetical economic adviser takes no position. Yet there might well be a conflict between pursuing the economist's two goals and satisfying a sense of justice in distributing economic goods. Even if it could be shown that putting the cost of all accidents on drivers would minimize the net cost of accidents, the justice of making motorists as a class poorer would still be open to serious challenge.

In retrospect, the harvest from being patient with economic analysis proves to be somewhat ironic. In the situation in which his analysis is most refreshing, the economist tells us that the liability issue is not worth arguing about except possibly as a strategy for compulsory accident insurance; and in the other situation, where he stresses that the legal rule does affect the allocation of resources, his analysis at best yields indecisive clues as to the proper answer. To exaggerate only a little, when the economist is helpful he says that the legal problem is not worth arguing about; when he finds the legal problem consequential, he cannot be helpful in fashioning a solution. And in any event, the two criteria borrowed from him do not profess to touch issues of equity that are the ultimate concern of the law.

10

We have argued that there is no basis in common sense, economic analysis or in justice for placing the cost of all accidents on motorists. In working through this argument we have not devoted much attention to the actual mechanics of liability insurance in our society. The fact, of course, is that most motorists carry liability insurance; and for convenience in further analysis we will assume that all motorists insure under a compulsory liability scheme.[135] The proponent of a compensation plan may now claim that there has been a hiatus in our analysis as it bears on putting costs on motorists. With compulsory insurance assumed, costs, whatever the legal principle on which they are allocated, will be

---

[135] And further that there is no problem of "under insurance"; see notes 51 and 55 *supra*.

experienced by motorists only through charges for insurance premiums. Liability insurance necessarily ties the fate of any one motorist to the conduct of a mass of other motorists. It is this pooling of risks which it might be argued impeaches some aspects of our former analysis.

A few salient features about auto liability insurance now become relevant. Perhaps the most significant for our purposes is that insurance rates by and large do not discriminate among motorists. It is only a moderate exaggeration to say that liability risks are so homogenized that, with some important exceptions, all motorists are charged as though they represented the same risk.[136] To the extent that the rates do discriminate, the most widely used criteria are impersonal actuarial categories, such as extremes of age, family composition, geographical location and type of vehicle. In the limited instances in which the discrimination is based on the safety history of the particular motorist, the relevant criterion is simply accident involvement.[137] Neither in recording the accident involvement of the individual motorist nor in making the comparisons between various classes of motorists is attention paid to the incidence of fault. The insurance industry could scarcely do otherwise, given the need for a sound statistical base in establishing differential premium rates. In short, liability insurers in allocating costs among the insured appear to think in strict liability terms.

Undoubtedly the current formulas for allocating costs among insureds present some substantial issues of policy.[138] At the moment, however, the question is simply whether such considerations add any force to the case for burdening motorists with the cost of compensating victims who are ineligible for recovery at common law. Several aspects of our earlier analysis need to be re-examined in this connection. But first we must look at a new argument in support of strict liability which emerges in the insurance context.

When we turn to the setting of insurance rates, does not our whole quest for a proper basis for handling accident costs become absurd? If we are willing to tolerate gross arbitrariness in allocating cost *among* insureds, so the new argument runs, are we not being ultra-fastidious in worrying so much about who should bear the cost of accident losses not shifted off victims today? What is involved here are two wholly distinct variables which affect the premium charged the individual motorist. One

---

136 Morris, *supra* note 129; Peck, *Comparative Negligence and Automobile Liability Insurance*, 58 MICH. L. REV. 689 (1960).

137 Under the omnibus clause, an accident involving the omnibus insured is charged under the usual practice against the record of the principal insured.

138 How many refinements to introduce in classifying insureds is a general problem for all types of insurance. See JOSEPHSON, DISCRIMINATION, A STUDY OF RECENT DEVELOPMENTS IN AMERICAN LIFE INSURANCE (1960).

is the total cost to be borne by the insurance pool; the other is the formula for sharing this total cost among the individual motorists who contribute to the pool. In effect the critic urges that although both variables significantly affect the premium level, in our analysis we have been obsessed with policy concerning the first and have been indifferent to the second. A simple illustration may sharpen the issue. Let us assume that a given motorist now pays a premium of $100. A shift to a compensation plan would increase his premium to $150. Absent a plan, if more sensitive discriminations were made in setting rates, his premium would be $25. The critic asserts that we are more concerned about the 50% increase called for by a plan than by the 300% overpayment which typifies the existing system. Since we are willing to tolerate the larger inequity, how can we rationally insist upon being so pure about the other?

We readily grant that there may be serious injustices in setting insurance rates, and that for all we know they may bulk larger from the point of view of an individual insured than the consequences of moving to a compensation plan. But despite the elaborateness of the critic's argument, it is still true that two wrongs do not make a right. All that the argument amounts to is a call for doing something to improve the standard for setting of rates among the insureds. We would agree.

There is an interesting variant of this argument. The crux is that as long as liability is keyed to fault, our insurance system is tied to an insurable event which is unmanageable. It is impossible to set rates among insureds fairly since it is impractical to take fault into account in establishing subcategories of risks. In its most general form the argument is that the insurable event provides a new criterion for the selection of a liability rule. Since, as we have said, the auto insurance industry seems to think in strict liability terms in setting rates, the law should adopt a liability system which is as congenial as possible to the insurance mechanism. Presumably strict liability alone would fit the prescription.

The underlying assumption here is not tenable. No one has the information which is needed to make the judgment that the combination of compulsory liability insurance with liability keyed to fault necessarily will have the consequence of producing an improper allocation of insurance costs among insureds. In order to make that judgment it would be necessary to know in advance the distribution of fault among drivers in causing accidents. Such information seems to be inaccessible, at least at present. If the distribution were known, there is nothing about the insurance system which in theory would prevent that data from being used in discriminating among insureds. In the present state of ignorance, the system at least randomizes the chances of error involved in not having categories based on fault. Further, auto insurance today so little exploits the possibility of using differential premiums based on already accessible factors that it is extravagantly premature to urge a shift to strict liability in order to allow for an improvement in the justice of allocating premiums among the insureds. Finally, it is not true that any one liability principle provides an insurable event that is more congenial to the art of insurance than does any other liability principle. "Sound" pricing of insurance only requires being able to measure and project the incidence of the insurable event in a given population. One insurable event is as manageable as another.

So much for using insurance mechanics to argue for strict liability. We move now to a re-examination of our earlier analysis in the light of insurance considerations.

It will be recalled that one economic goal we accepted was having consumers face up to proper full costs in choosing among alternatives.[139] The argument has been advanced that insurance succeeds not only in spreading costs but perhaps even more significantly it also succeeds in educating users about costs. On this educational feature it might be possible to suggest another rationale for placing the cost of the additional coverage under a plan on motorists. In discussing the goal of realistic consumer choice, we pointed out that regrettably it was impossible to tell whether the cost of an accident not due to the fault of the driver was a cost of using autos, or of being a pedestrian, or of just living in society. Assuming a wide use of liability insurance, the new proposal would be to place some fraction, say one-half, of such cost on motorists in order to confront them with it as a cost of operating a car. The assumption is that it is plausible that some part of the cost of all auto accidents belongs to motoring as an activity, and that we cannot be far wrong if we settle for one-half.[140] It is then argued that consumers are presented with more realistic cost alternatives where half of these losses is made a cost of motoring than where none is, especially since a car is involved in all auto accidents while pedestrians or other factors need not be present in every instance.

Such arguments are ingenious but not persuasive. The whole point to this aspect of economic analysis is that resources should be allocated in response to consumer voting and that the allocation should not be distorted by confronting consumers with improper cost alternatives. Assigning some arbitrary fraction of accident losses to motoring does not necessarily reduce such distortion. It might sound prudent to split the

---

139 See section 9, *supra* pages 54 *et seq.*

140 We borrow here from an argument made to us by Guido Calabresi of the Yale Law School. We understand that he will soon be publishing his own analysis of many of the issues we have covered.

loss in two, but there is no way of knowing whether charging motorists 50% of the loss brings about more or less of a distortion than would charging them nothing for losses—or charging them everything.

It will also be recalled that a second economic goal which we accepted in our prior analysis was that of maximizing output through minimizing waste.[141] In the matter of auto accidents, pursuit of this objective would dictate placing the cost of accident losses on that class of persons who would take steps to reduce accidents by the least costly means. We recognized that this was simply a different way of approaching the not unfamiliar problem of deterrence. We concluded that tort sanctions probably had little impact on the quality of driving conduct; but we observed that if deterrence of accidents were taken as a serious goal for liability policy it appeared that the common law combination of negligence and contributory negligence was most likely to maximize whatever deterrent potential there might be. We have now reached a convenient place to consider what bearing use of liability insurance has on these possibilities for reducing waste.

The obvious point is that insurance may dampen whatever stimulus to deterrence there may be in liability rules. To the extent that the pooling of risks for insurance purposes homogenizes insureds, as it does by and large under current practices, it can only blunt the impact of liability on driving conduct. But, at most, all that such considerations do is to weaken a very faint argument on behalf of the fault liability principle. They in no way strengthen the affirmative case for a compensation plan.

Such discussion serves to remind us once more that there is much room for experimentation and greater daring in setting insurance rates for the sake of creating more deterrent impact. From time to time insurance companies have experimented with classifications based on safe driving histories so as to give rate discounts to drivers who have good records from an insurance point of view. A well established English practice has been to offer a discount to a motorist where there has been no claim against his liability policy over stated periods, with the discount increasing for each successive claim-free period.[142] Certain companies in the United States have experimented with a demerit point system based on the presence or absence of moving traffic violations.[143] Recently there

141 See section 9, *supra* pages 54 *et seq.*

142 Netherton, *Highway Safety Under Differing Types of Liability Legislation,* 15 OHIO ST. L.J. 110, 123-24 (1954).

143 For example, the "Safe Driver Insurance Plan" initiated a few years ago in California. Under it each moving violation and each involvement in an auto accident, regardless of fault, is scored as a point against the insured. Motorists with one point

have been suggestions that deterrence might be increased by use of a mandatory deductible provision which would take loss off the victim but leave part of it on the negligent driver.[144] In general, however, the whole experience in the United States with such rating devices has not been very encouraging. Premium differences have, for the most part, been relatively small and unglamorous, and further elaboration along these lines, it is feared, may tend to complicate or embarrass the insurers in the ready marketing of their product. The rate differences, moreover, have usually been in the form of reductions in premiums for safe driving and have been advertised and understood as rewards and not as penalties. We suspect that these differentials serve not so much to affect driving conduct as to establish fairer rates for those who are the careful drivers anyway. But whether or not more effective arrangements can be devised, the topic has little bearing on the main theme of our analysis. The potentiality for differentiating premiums in terms of safe driving in no respect depends on changing from the common law system to a compensation plan.

Two final details. There may be some additional economies in shifting from insurance under a fault system to insurance under a compensation plan. Some of the diseconomies which exist today in the processing of claims because of the duplication of insurance coverage could be eliminated.[145] These savings, however, are not likely to be large enough to affect significantly our previous analysis of the possibility of financing a compensation plan through internal economies.[146]

It is appropriate to take another glance at the social security approach to a plan in this insurance context. The fact that now becomes visible is that the tax to finance social security coverage of accidents could be either flat or progressive, but it could not exploit differentials of the kind we have just discussed in connection with liability insurance carried by motorists. In utilizing a socal security approach there would be no way of tying costs imposed on individuals to their safety records or their accident exposure. To the extent that otherwise obtainable deterrence is sacrificed, the social security model loses in attractiveness.

This digression on liability insurance has, we think, shown that nothing is changed significantly when we explicitly take account of how insurance costs are shared among the insureds. Neither the risk pooling aspects of

---

pay the regular rate. Those with no points pay 20% less, and those with more than one point pay progressively more up to a maximum of 100% for five or more points.

144 Oppenheimer, *Insured to Kill*, 1953 Ins. L.J. 14.

145 Compare EHRENZWEIG, "FULL AID" INSURANCE (1954).

146 See section 8, *supra* pages 44 *et seq.*

insurance nor its other characteristics alter the balance of the argument for a compensation plan.

11

We have noted that, generally speaking, compensation plans have two major targets: elimination of some or all the gaps in coverage and improvement in the timing of payment to victims.[147] The main policy implications raised by extension of coverage have called for a detailed analysis of four possible ways for financing the cost of the additional coverage. We have now finished that, the major, segment of our discussion. We are ready to turn to the policy implications of the second target of compensation plans—expediting payment of compensation to victims.

If the timing of payments to victims is a criterion, the common law system of compensation comes out badly. Recent studies of auto accident law in action have vividly documented how clumsily the common law often times its payments.[148] But the common law was not set up as a system to finance payment of the urgent and immediate needs of victims. From the beginning it has been regarded as a system for ultimately allocating the cost of accidents. It is true that its shortcomings in paying compensation promptly are aggravated by court congestion and the dilatory tactics of those participating in the process. The deficiency of the common law as a first aid mechanism, however, goes far beyond such considerations; it is intrinsic to its liability for fault rationale. That principle necessarily clouds the handling of a great number of claims by putting liability in doubt. The sad consequence from the point of view of the welfare of the victim is that current payments, to cover emergency needs, might well not be forthcoming until the ultimate liability issue has been resolved.[149]

The experience with workmen's compensation is instructive. Although there is still ample controversy over claims, almost all of it concerns the final amount of disability awards and not interim payments for medical and emergency expenses. No conceivable improvement in the common law could speed up its payments enough to meet this challenge from a compensation plan.

Prompt payment, all other things being equal, is an indisputable advantage. Does recognition of this advantage change the balance of policy arguments on auto compensation plans? Or is the advantage of

---

[147] See section 5, *supra* pages 30 *et seq.*

[148] Especially the Conard study. See note 12 *supra.*

[149] A familiar strain on the personal injury bar in congested court areas is financing badly injured claimants while the litigation is pending. ZEISEL, KALVEN & BUCHHOLZ, DELAY IN THE COURT xxiii (1959).

promptness, like the advantage of additional coverage, one which can be had only at a price?

On reflection it will be seen that there necessarily is a price, but that it is curiously complicated to trace. The key fact is that prompt payment of accident claims can be had only by increasing coverage of victims. Promptness depends on making payment of claims, or some component of them, virtually automatic, and this in turn depends on simplifying the liability profile by eliminating distinctions, and in particular that between fault and no fault. The additional coverage of course involves an additional cost. To complete the circle, the price for enabling prompt payment is the cost of financing the additional coverage. The issue can now be more fully stated: Does the advantage of prompt payment alter in any way the assessment we already have made of the cost question?

We shall explore the question by revisiting briefly each of the four alternatives for financing additional coverage.

All along we have agreed that wider coverage of accident victims is an attractive idea, but we have insisted that the question of who properly and justly should pay the cost must be confronted. A compensation plan becomes even more attractive when we consider its feature of prompt payment of medical and emergency expenses to all victims. However, there is nothing about the desirability of having claims paid promptly that increases the persuasiveness of the case for placing new costs on motorists. Our earlier analysis of putting added costs on motorists is unaffected.

Similarly, there is no need to modify our analysis of financing additional costs through effectuating economies in handling claims by switching from the common law to a compensation plan. Nothing about promptness in payment increases the likelihood that the cost problem can be solved merely by such economies.[150]

In considering the possibility of financing the added cost by reallocating damages among victims, we do find a new stimulus to analysis. When we examined the case for financing coverage of new victims in this manner, we encountered, it may be recalled, two major difficulties: It was hard to see why more deserving victims should be asked to surrender part of their awards to less deserving victims, without getting any benefit in return; and it was hard to explain why, if damage awards are to be lowered, the insured motorists are not entitled to a rebate.[151] Both of these difficulties are lessened in the new context. The decisive

---

[150] There may be some economies. Delay in making payments is itself likely to entail costs. Further, if payments are prompt, it may be easier to integrate a program of accident insurance and a program of liability insurance.

[151] See section 6, *supra* pages 32 *et seq.*

point is that, unlike expanded coverage which would benefit only new victims, prompt payment would benefit all victims. Thus, old victims —those compensable at common law—might be seen as getting a quid pro quo by accepting reduced awards in return for greatly increased promptness in payment. Moreover, the insured motorists would have no claim to a rebate in this context. Awards, it is assumed, are to be reduced not because damages are too high but because payment is too slow. If the image is that the previously eligible victims are willing to negotiate with the newly covered victims—and to take less in order to take sooner—their bargain is no concern of the motorists.

We cannot resist underscoring how striking this argument for a plan is. Motorists cannot complain because they are not called on to pay more and they have no claim to a rebate. Old victims as a class apparently have no cause to complain since they gain the advantage of prompt payment. New victims, of course, end up being covered. We seem to have only winners and no losers.

But of course the matter is somewhat more complicated. On further analysis there are at least three reasons for thinking that not all of the old victims would be delighted with the bargain made on their behalf. People do react differently if confronted with the choice of taking a small but certain amount now or gambling on a larger but less certain payment in the future.[152] Further, all victims are offered the same bargain, regardless of how good a common law claim they are forced to give up. And it is obvious that inasmuch as the economic circumstances of victims vary, so will their need for prompt payment of medical and emergency expenses. In short, there is still some force in the argument that in making a reallocation of damages to finance a plan, we would be transferring money from more deserving to less deserving victims.

This vision of a bargain also has some embarrassments which we have met before.[153] Any bargain which assumes that no new costs will be put on motorists is treacherous because, as noted earlier, once a plan is adopted it will be difficult to determine whether the burden on motorists is being increased. It is only too likely that the burden on motorists will be increased gradually so that the principle involved in rescinding the bargain can never be debated.

These last considerations lead easily to the final point to be re-examined—financing the additional costs along social security lines. On

[152] The experience under the Family Plan insurance scheme, discussed in section 4, *supra* pages 27 *et seq.*, is instructive here; except for very small claims, few victims were attracted by the opportunity to trade their contingent claim to payment in the future for a certain, albeit smaller, payment now.

[153] See section 6, *supra* pages 32 *et seq.*

our view the case for handling compensation payments through a social security system is strengthened when prompt payment of medical and emergency expenses is taken as a major objective. Welfare then becomes a dominant theme. It would seem more congenial to switch the discourse into a welfare framework and to recognize that the common law categories of thought are wholly out of place in such a context. The ease of accommodating a rationale for prompt payment to victims under a social security approach underscores how artificial and unduly ingenious is the case for bribing old victims with prompt payment in order to cover new victims. If one is serious about the overriding importance of speedy payment to victims, the most appropriate approach would seem to be extension of social security measures.

At this point we repeat the observation we already have made about the provinciality of auto compensation plans as welfare measures. If it is important to provide speedy medical and emergency payments to those who suffer the misfortune of auto accidents, it must be equally important to provide equally prompt payments to those who suffer comparable misfortunes from other causes.

12

We have now completed an examination of what we would regard as the main issues of policy concerning auto compensation plans. We are aware that we have not discussed many points that are salient in the literature. To anyone acquainted with the literature on plans, it will be apparent that we have insisted on imposing our own analytic structure on the topic. Thus we have said hardly anything about court congestion, the maintenance of the jury system, the status of the trial bar, and the prospect of further state intervention in the insurance industry.[154] It is to such points as these that we now turn as a kind of extended postscript.

On our view these points concern by-products and side effects of adopting a compensation plan. In judging the merits of any large scale reform, it is of course relevant to weigh in the balance the various collateral effects which can be anticipated. Much of the discussion of compensation plans, however, seems concerned not with the attractiveness or unattractiveness of these effects, but rather with a type of real-politic speculation on how they affect the likelihood that the reform will, as a political matter, be acceptable. It may well be that, because of the probable effects of a plan on the trial bar and the private insurance industry, no plan will

---

[154] Or, to add still another, the problem of the out-of-state motorist.

in the foreseeable future muster enough political support to gain adoption. The experience of the past thirty years following the first announcement of the Columbia plan suggests that resistance to this sort of a plan is strong indeed; and no study is needed to demonstrate that there is a remarkably great gap between the enthusiasm of the majority of the academic specialists for a plan and the negative reaction of state legislatures and public officials. The most telling evidence of the political power of the insurance industry is found in the history of even so modest a reform as compulsory liability insurance for all motorists. It has been adopted only in a handful of states and this after a gap of twenty-five years before another state followed the lead of Massachusetts.[155] If the problem is one of prediction, an always risky venture, the outlook for compensation plans impresses us as being not bright.

We mention prospects for the future because, as is so often the case in discussion of policy, there is a tendency to elide prediction into treatment of the merits. In the federal tax field, we have long been familiar with the phenomenon that certain major reforms are almost never discussed seriously since it is believed that they have no reasonable prospect of being adopted; active discussion tends to be limited to minor changes at the edges of the rules.[156] It is a prerogative of academic analysis to define the realm of the possible more generously than need the man of affairs. Under this license we turn to consider possible side effects of compensation plans, advisedly ignoring how these affect the likelihood of a plan being adopted.

One feature of a plan often urged as a positive advantage is that it would provide a remedy for court congestion.[157] Personal injury litigation constitutes the overwhelming fraction of all cases in large urban court systems, and since the auto accident looms large among the sources of personal injury, there is no doubt that taking auto cases out of the court system pursuant to a plan would dramatically reduce the congestion problem in urban courts. It would be difficult to imagine any single step likely to have more decisive impact on court delay. Nonetheless, we would reject this as an independent argument on behalf of a plan. Court congestion, although a stubborn and serious matter today, is surely not an intrinsic characteristic of the common law system, and many areas of

[155] GREGORY & KALVEN, CASES ON TORTS 733-42 (1959).

[156] The lack of practical discussion or action engendered by the radical and critical analysis of the federal income tax law in SIMONS, PERSONAL INCOME TAXATION (1938) and FEDERAL TAX REFORM (1950) furnishes perhaps a classic instance. See also Blum, *Federal Income Tax Reform—Twenty Questions*, 41 TAXES 672 (1963).

[157] ZEISEL, KALVEN & BUCHHOLZ, DELAY IN THE COURT (1959). Compare Hofstadter, *Alternative Proposal to the Compensation Plan*, 1956 INS. L.J. 331; Hofstadter, *A Proposed Automobile Accident Compensation Plan*, 328 ANNALS 53 (March 1960).

the United States do not today experience it.[158] The court congestion problem should be dealt with directly and on its own terms; it should not be permitted to serve as a justification for radical changes in the substantive law. Unless persuaded of the merits of a plan, court congestion apart, one cannot endorse a plan simply because it will help with court delay.[159]

A plan can also be expected to have important consequences for the contemporary trial scene and especially for the trial judge, the personal injury bar and the civil jury. Under a plan, a major group of cases would be withdrawn from the trial process and turned over to an administrative process. It is widely feared that the result would be a kind of technological unemployment for the trial judge and the trial lawyer. It is becoming familiar at bar association gatherings to hear some leader of the bar sound Jeremiah-like warnings about the dark future of the bench and bar under plans. But it is easy to overstate the drama of these changes. Probably few trial judges in urban courts would be literally unemployed after the switch to a plan; and, as we saw earlier, the negotiating and settlement functions of lawyers, which are today the lion's share of the bar's personal injury activities, would still be in demand.[160] The adoption of a plan, however, would mark a long step away from the centrality of litigation as the traditional method of resolving stubborn controversies.

The impact of a plan on the jury system presents for us a more interesting issue. Under a plan a major part of the contemporary function of the civil jury would disappear.[161] Despite the fact that one *could* have a plan which retained the jury trial for controversies not disposed of by negotiation, all plans appear to transfer such residual controversy into administrative channels. This readiness to eliminate the jury probably has several sources: the convenience of borrowing from the existing workmen's compensation format, the hope of speeding up the process of

---

[158] See the annual calendar studies of the Institute of Judicial Administration, which cover approximately 100 courts throughout the United States.

[159] Compare Zeisel, *The Jury and Court Delay*, 328 ANNALS 46 (March 1960).

[160] See section 7, *supra* pages 40 *et seq.*

[161] Under most proposed plans the jury would disappear altogether. Under the Saskatchewan plan, it is retained in the common law action over for damages in excess of the schedule. Under the special English combination of social insurance and tort remedy, it is available in theory. However, by an independent reform, England has since World War II greatly reduced the jurisdiction of the civil jury. See DEVLIN, TRIAL BY JURY (1956); Friedman, *Social Insurance and the Principles of Tort Liability*, 63 HARV. L. REV. 241 (1949); Grad, *Recent Developments in Automobile Accident Compensation*, 50 COLUM. L. REV. 300, 329 (1950); *cf.* James, *The Columbia Study of Compensation for Automobile Accidents: An Unanswered Challenge*, 59 COLUM. L. REV. 408, 420 (1959).

adjudication, and the respect for administrative expertise. It is worth observing that in some ways the case for establishing an administrative agency seems upside down here. Today the standard argument for having an administrative agency, such as the Securities and Exchange Commission or the Federal Communications Commission, is that the regulation of a complex technical field is involved, requiring special experience and skill and the need to develop a set of structured rules. The role of a commission under an auto compensation plan would be startlingly different. It would face questions of historical fact as to whether the event giving rise to the claim actually happened, and questions of medical fact as to the nature and extent of injury and disability. The liability issue, and to some degree the damage issue, would be considerably simpler than the ones we have traditionally left to the jury at common law.[162] We thus would appear to be following the curious sequence of first simplifying the issues and then shifting them from a layman to an expert tribunal.

The basis for dropping the jury may come from a different corner. Under common law the jury is entrusted with two great issues: to draw the negligence line and to put an individual dollar price on damages in a particular case. These both pre-eminently require the common sense and feel of the community, which it has been the special genius of the jury to supply. By its strict liability rule a plan would make unnecessary the negligence discrimination, and by its damages schedule a plan would make unnecessary the individualized pricing of damages. The reason then why a plan can do without a jury is that it does not require these distinctive strengths of the jury.

Whatever the reasons for dropping the jury, retaining it under a plan never seems to get explicit consideration. There perhaps is a lesson here in the process by which major social changes are brought to pass in our society. For two hundred years the merits of the jury system in civil cases have been strongly attacked and strongly defended; for almost the whole time it has remained peculiarly immune to change in the United States. Yet, as in the case of the workmen's compensation acts, auto compensation plans would result in sweeping away the jury in an important area of civil controversy. It may be that radical alteration in the use of juries in our society can come about only when the change is regarded as a minor facet of a program of substantive reform.

Indeed, if elimination of the jury were not taken for granted under auto compensation plans, the experience with workmen's compensation in some localities might well supply a lively defense for retaining the institution. The argument would be that the jury is protection against

---

[162] The liability issue will always be simpler. However, the damage issue may have its complexities; see section 6, *supra* pages 32 *et seq.*

corruption. An old point is involved. Conventionally the case for the jury has been thought strongest where there is reason to doubt the neutrality and integrity of the judge. It seems to us that the case loses none of its force where there is reason to doubt the neutrality and integrity of administrators who transfer large sums of money through adjudication. The protective role of the jury very likely is even more needed vis-à-vis administrators than vis-à-vis judges.[163]

We consider next the impact of auto plans on the insurance industry. Its spokemen have been untiring in alerting society to the dangers they perceive. In assessing the industry's brief, it is difficult to separate out the objections which go to compensation plans from those which go to compulsory liability insurance. The industry's position on compulsory insurance is an oft told story and need not be repeated in detail.[164] We would note only that there appears to be a slight suggestion of perversity in the industry's resistance to a governmental move designed to make everyone buy its product.[165] What interests us now is to see whether there are any objections to compensation plans from the insurance industry's point of view that are distinctive to plans and not simply repetitive of its objections to compulsory insurance.

The arguments offered publicly to date have been unfocused and not in response to any particular auto plan. They have left the general impression that the case largely reduces to cliches about moving further

163 This conclusion is based on conversations with experienced compensation lawyers in large metropolitan areas.

164 See HENSLEY, COMPETITION, REGULATION AND THE PUBLIC INTEREST IN NON-LIFE INSURANCE 116-33 (1962); Knepper, *Law, Insurance and the Automobile Accident Victim: A Defense of the Present Legal System*, 29 J. INS. 159 (1962); Kramer, *Fallacies of a Compensation Plan for Automobile Accident Litigation*, 26 INS. COUNSEL J. 420 (1959); Lilly in *Compensation for Automobile Accidents: A Symposium*, 32 COLUM. L. REV. 785, 803-12 (1932); Sherman, *Grounds for Opposing the Automobile Accident Compensation Plan*, 3 LAW & CONTEMP. PROB. 598 (1936).

165 A special commission reporting in 1929 on the Massachusetts experience with compulsory liability insurance, observed: "The state requires its citizens to wear clothes on the street, and to a certain limited extent even on the stage, or at least the state would lock them up if they did not, but it does not follow that the state may 'properly' establish a state clothing monopoly to 'supply its citizens' with the clothing which 'it requires' them to wear and force them to buy their clothes of the state. Yet the requirements that clothes be worn in public applies to all citizens except babies, while the requirement of motor vehicle insurance applies only to a part of the citizens. We see no more justification for requiring a man or woman to buy state insurance, when he or she prefers to buy private insurance in a responsible company, than there is for requiring a man or woman to buy all his or her clothes from the state. If there is legislative power to make such a requirement, we believe it is one of those powers, like the power to move the State House dome into the Frog Pond, which should not be exercised." REPORT OF THE SPECIAL COMMISSION TO STUDY COMPULSORY MOTOR VEHICLE LIABILITY INSURANCE AND RELATED MATTERS, 15 MASS. L.Q. No. 3 p. 175 (1930).

down the road to serfdom. To go deeper we need to speculate about what particular threats distress the industry.

Two prophecies of doom for the private liability insurance industry are to be distinguished. One is that adoption of a plan will slowly but inevitably lead to ever broader regulation of the industry until it becomes simply a private arm of government in collecting and distributing funds. There is little new or helpful that can be said about how well grounded is the fear of gradual encroachment. The evidence under workmen's compensation leans the other way; after half a century of experience in the majority of states there exists a lively private industry of insurance carriers.[166] The other prediction is that from the outset the very design of certain compensation plans will preclude any significant role for private industry. This clearly would be so if the plan took the form of a welfare scheme for potential victims, financed through taxation, and administered along the lines of our social security system. Those who on other grounds would rate the social security model as best must confront the question whether its advantages are sufficient to offset the disadvantages of curtailing the private insurance industry and increasing the role of government.

Short of a plan which eliminated the need for private insurance altogether, the industry concern may be that a plan would call for use of state funds to supplement the compensation pool raised through private insurance premiums. Such a subsidy would place the industry in the position of being a partner with the state, causing it to be regarded as a trustee administering state funds in handling claims. From the industry's point of view, the prospect is a stifling degree of supervision over the administrative and selling costs which the industry could charge against premiums collected.

Even absent a contribution of state funds, the type of insurance required for a compensation plan is likely to lead to a higher degree of standardization for the industry. Public authorities presumably would prescribe the coverage, policy limits, payment conditions, and settlement terms and procedures. As a consequence, there would be far less room for competition between companies on the basis of premiums, service or policy terms. And most dramatically, there would be economic and political pressures to redesign the marketing practices of the industry to accommodate this increased standardization and to avoid the diseconomies associated with the present methods of merchandising liability insurance.

To overgeneralize, the possible threats of plans range from eliminating

---

166 See DODD, ADMINISTRATION OF WORKMEN'S COMPENSATION (1936).

at the outset the entire role of the industry down to rendering obsolete the practices that have most markedly characterized it in the past as a private industry. The perceptions of any of these changes can account for the opposition of the industry to plans. Among these degrees of state intervention we see an important difference. The strength of the industry might be curtailed through regulation, but so long as it remains outside the government the industry could continue to be an important island of private power. It is a characteristic of insurance company arguments against plans to elide this distinction and, as a result, to move too rapidly from the danger of increased regulation to the danger of "nationalization."

We should again stress that for us the relevant question as to side effects is not whether they will irritate certain groups in the society and cause the mounting of political opposition to a plan; the question rather is whether they constitute changes which must be weighed impartially in deciding upon over-all policy. But we should caution that in the case of effects on the insurance industry, it is especially difficult to separate out the irritants—such as loss of profits or prestige—from the genuine costs to society.

13

It is obvious that we have been able to talk about auto compensation plans at considerable length without directly discussing any plan in particular—the Saskatchewan Plan,[167] the Columbia Plan,[168] the Green Plan,[169] the Keeton and O'Connell Plan,[170] or the Ehrenzweig Plan.[171] We are not guilty, however, of playing Hamlet without Hamlet. All of the particular plans are hybrids as to financing the coverage for additional victims.[172] Some of these plans may well be defensible, if not admirable, as political compromises. But we would insist that one should not confuse universes. Our commitment has been to mapping and exploring the basic policy issues that any plan must entail.[173]

---

[167] See note 157 *supra*; GREGORY & KALVEN, CASES ON TORTS 757-60 (1959); Rokes, *The Saskatchewan Plan*, 29 J. INS. 373 (1962).

[168] See note 6 *supra*.

[169] See note 13 *supra*.

[170] See note 2 *supra*.

[171] See note 9 *supra*.

[172] Thus, the Columbia Plan both reduces common law damages and places the additional costs of coverage on drivers, combining the routes we discuss in sections 6 and 9 respectively. The most complex financing scheme is found in EHRENZWEIG, "FULL AID" INSURANCE (1954); see Kalven, Book Review, 33 TEXAS L. REV. 778 (1955).

[173] We suspect that whatever consensus there may be for preferring a plan over the common law depends in considerable part upon the circumstance that the

We come at last to the end of that long and winding road of analysis. From this vantage point it may be appropriate to try a brief summary statement of how the case for an auto compensation plan looks to us now.

We of course find attractive the two main objectives of plans: to compensate all victims and to provide medical and emergency expense payments promptly. Nor can there be any argument but that the common law fails to achieve either of these. It does not achieve the first because it intends as a matter of policy to leave some victims uncompensated; and it cannot as a matter of practice achieve the second inasmuch as it limits liability to fault and hence subjects that issue to controversy.

In analyzing plans it quickly becomes apparent that the old common law issue of liability translates into a question of costs. Changing the form of the question does not cause the underlying issue to evaporate. Any plan requires coverage of additional victims in order to achieve its twin objectives. Additional coverage of victims means additional cost. The central policy problem, in weighing the merits of plans, is: How is this additional cost to be defrayed?

The solution most frequently suggested is to put the cost on motorists, and thus to pose the issue of strict liability versus negligence. We have been unable to find a satisfactory justification for imposing the additional cost on motorists. Once the fault criterion has been laid aside, we see no basis in common sense for charging them. We are unimpressed with arguments based on the perception of an irreversible historical trend. And we derive no support for charging mototrists from economic analysis of the superior risk bearer formula.

But this is by no means the end of the argument. There are three other ways of financing the cost of additional coverage. At least in theory this means that there are alternative methods of moving to an auto compensation plan without obligating motorists as a class to pay more than they now pay under common law. It is therefore not necessary or helpful to tie analysis of compensation plans to the debate over strict liability versus negligence.

The first alternative is to seek financing through economies in handling claims expected to follow from simplifying the criteria for making payments to victims. As a solution this has the great appeal of appearing to be painless to all concerned, except possibly to the lawyers whose fees would be substantially reduced. This approach, however, is not apt to

---

advocates have not been required to agree on which of the four routes to a plan is proper or best.

take us as far as is hoped. At best the magnitude of the savings from internal economies alone is likely to fall far short of requirements, and at worst it is likely to be offset by an increase in claims consciousness.

The second alternative is to generate the financing by reallocating awards among victims. The arresting aspect of this approach is that while motorists remain unaffected by the switch to a plan, the victims who would be eligible for recovery at common law are materially affected. As long as the focus is on providing additional coverage, such a reallocation looks like a stratagem for taking something away from more deserving victims in order to give it to less deserving victims. When, however, the focus is on improving the time of payment for medical and emergency expenses, there emerges a quid pro quo to the old victims who, as a class, are compelled to accept smaller awards in order to get quicker payments.

It might be possible to finance a plan by drawing on each of these last two sources. The result would be a plan which, in theory, would not alter the position of motorists, would not drive too hard a bargain with old victims, and would not make unrealistic demands on effectuating economies in handling claims. On this avowedly eclectic approach the full formula for producing a plan would run as follows:[174] (1) Take no more from motorists than in the absence of a plan. (2) Maximize the economies in handling claims. (3) Tentatively set the award level so as to reflect these economies through lowering the gross awards without reducing the take-home sums. (4) Adjust the tentative award level downward so that the old victims give up enough in take-home sums to cover any gap in satisfying the claims of new victims.[175]

For a brief moment this compromise seems to realize the philosopher's dream of a political solution which achieves the common good—a solution in which there is an adjustment of self interests in a manner that is mutually satisfactory to each participant. On further inspection, however, the dream tends to fade. There is the doubt that, as a political matter, the promise to the motorists can be kept; there is the doubt that the savings through economies in handling claims will be substantial enough to avoid a harsh bargain with the old victims; there is the high likelihood that some old victims, either because of the certainty of their claim at common law or because of their comfortable economic position, will in any event find the bargain detrimental; there is the difficulty of communicating the rationale for the compromise to a wide enough

---

174 For present purposes, we need not specify how damages will be allocated. Any of the five variations discussed in section 6, *supra* pages 32 et seq., will suffice here.

175 This may sound more complicated than it is. All it involves is combining two sources of financing: economies and reallocating damages.

public to enlist sufficient political support; and there is the difficulty of translating the compromise formula into a concrete plan.

But the main challenge comes from quite another quarter. The rival is the final alternative for financing the additional cost. It will be recalled that the last approach is not to shift losses directly but to put the burden on all victims as a class—a class which is co-extensive with the entire population. The image is of compulsory accident insurance for everyone; but in reality so wide a scheme of accident insurance would require use of the taxing mechanism to collect premiums, producing what can be viewed as an extension of social security.

The greatest strength of this approach is that it frames the problem candidly and coherently. From the very beginning the proponents of plans have insisted that the auto accident be viewed as an instance of human misfortune calling for a welfare remedy. When the situation is looked at in this manner, it immediately becomes apparent that the problem is bigger than that which the proponents started out to solve. The welfare universe is not limited to victims of auto accidents but includes victims of all other kinds of human misfortune. We can think of no ground for singling out the misfortune of auto accident victims for special welfare treatment.

The social security perspective also has the merit of bringing to the surface the profound question of why the state should do anything about human misfortunes. We infer that those who urge the state to intervene have mixed motives. To some extent they favor sumptuary legislation in behalf of prudence. They are willing to restrict the power of the individual to choose because they distrust every man's capacity to make prudent judgments about privately carrying accident insurance. But more important, they are concerned over the financial ability of people to absorb misfortune. They see that by no means is everyone prosperous enough to buy adequate insurance against misfortune. The attraction of financing protection through the tax mechanism is that the necessary funds can be collected on some progressive tax basis, so that the richer will pay the costs for the poorer.[176] Intervention by the state thus is sought in order to mitigate the evils of poverty. We are tempted to hazard the grand generalization that at the root of most of our major social issues lies the concern with what is thought to be poverty.[177] The automobile compensation plan is no exception.

While social security provides a candid and coherent approach to the

[176] Compare section 9, *supra* pages 54 *et seq.*

[177] See BLUM & KALVEN, THE UNEASY CASE FOR PROGRESSIVE TAXATION (1953); compare Kalven & Rosenfield, *Minow Should Watch His Step in the Wasteland*, Fortune, Oct. 1962, p. 116.

problem of the accident victim, it leaves unanswered the common law's main question of justice. In addressing itself to the problem of the needy auto accident victim, the social security approach tells us that his claim to help from society should be on a par with the claims of others who suffer from misfortune. But it cannot tell us why losses caused by negligent motorists should not be shifted to these drivers. The common law's solution was to make negligent motorists poorer in order to compensate victims in full for their losses. The question is whether this is any less just because the needs of victims are provided for by society.

We would urge that, in theory, the case for shifting the loss to a faulty driver rather than leaving it with the victim or as a charge on society is not thereby impaired. Theory would thus call for drawing a distinction between responding immediately to the victim's needs and deciding at leisure under the fault principle who ultimately should bear the cost. Once the dust had settled on all payments, no one would have been compelled to pay taxes or premiums on insurance to cover losses caused him by the fault of another.

We may, however, be in an area where there is a wide gulf between the theoretical and the practical. The effort to be this pure in allocating costs according to fault presents formidable difficulties quite apart from any controversy about the appropriateness of fault as a criterion of liability.[178] To implement the suggested principle fully, the welfare fund would have to be allowed to recover over against the negligent actors. This complication raises two awful prospects: We can anticipate that motorists would then carry liability insurance against the threat of subrogation by the welfare fund, and the crucial equity would lie in adjustments between the insurance carriers and the welfare fund. And logic would seem to require that the welfare fund also be obligated to sue contributorily negligent victims.[179] The spectre of these two results might well induce us to accept the social security approach without a negligence rider.

A middle ground has been suggested. The social security approach could be used to underwrite relief for those in need without allowing any recovery over by the welfare fund. Victims of faulty drivers, however, would be left with their common law actions intact, subject only to deduction for welfare payments which they have received from the fund. Under such an arrangement, losses below a certain level would be borne by the public generally and would be allocated wholly without

---

[178] James, *Social Insurance and Tort Liability: The Problem of Alternative Remedies*, 27 N.Y.U.L. REV. 537 (1932); Note, *The Mitigating Effect on Damages of Social Welfare Programs*, 63 HARV. L. REV. 330 (1949).

[179] As indeed is the case in EHRENZWEIG, "FULL AID" INSURANCE (1954).

regard to fault, while losses above that level would be allocated according to the fault principle—some remaining on victims and some shifted to drivers as the principle dictated. This result is in effect the Saskatchewan plan. For those who have a wholesale lack of enthusiasm for the fault principle, retaining it in this context might well appear as a foolish luxury.

So much for the perplexities of either marrying or divorcing social security and fault.

The old common law issue of justice apart, the social security approach to the problem of the auto accident victim has some distinctive disadvantages of its own. If economic considerations have a bearing on accident causing behavior, this approach would seem to run the greatest risk of lessening deterrence. Neither drivers nor pedestrians would perceive any relationship between their taxes and their conduct in respect to automobiles. The approach also has the disadvantage of supplanting the private insurance industry in a major sector of its activities, and replacing it with taxation and government administration of welfare benefits. Such a development would add to the power of the government and weaken what now is an important private pool of power. Finally, the approach calls for one more—and perhaps an irreversible—reduction in the area of individual autonomy.

It is not comfortable for us to end by repeating all the well-aired objections to social security. We are aware that we are a long way from home. And it is no accident that we have travelled so far from the tort world from which we began. Private law cannot borrow goals from public law fields without accepting the obligation to make a proper public law analysis. In the case of automobile compensation plans, such an analysis shows that the special problem cannot be solved adequately without solving a larger problem. This much, at least, we have learned from this venture in applying public law perspectives to an important private law problem.

Topical Index